Delicious Direct Breads

Tempting, Tender & Tasty

We are a "home kitchen and bakery," and although we have owned a Country Inn with a Fine Dining Restaurant (that's a story for a different time), we are fully retired. We do not have any commercial endeavor, other than our writings. We cook and bake for pleasure, and delight in sharing with our neighbors and friends. Of course, Chef Tina runs "Tina's Kitchen," and since I manage the bakery in her kitchen, we refer to it as "Tina's Kitchen Bakery," or *TKB*. So even though we are not a commercial cooking/baking endeavor, we are a home enterprise that will soon celebrate its 55th anniversary.

We began writing about our bread making in 2013, which marked our 50th year of marriage. On May 18, 1963 at St Patrick's Catholic Church in Bay Shore, Long Island, we began a journey that continues to amaze us. We have been blessed with two daughters, grandchildren and great grandchildren, good friends, and many opportunities. We have been fortunate to travel about the world, as well as having seen and experienced the wonders of our own backyard.

We are retired, and enjoy having more time with family, friends and are fortunate to be in good health and be involved with all kinds of activities. Some of our favorite and frequent are: bridge; book club; home remodeling; furniture refinishing; gardening; traveling to old and new places; and sharing our love of cooking and baking bread with others.

Bettina (Tina) & Serge (Mickey)

Delicious Direct Breads

Tempting, Tender & Tasty

Serge & Bettina Doucette

Delicious Direct Breads: Tempting, Tender & Tasty
Copyright © 2018 By Serge R Doucette, Jr. and Bettina M. Doucette

ISBN-10: 1981368345
ISBN-13: 978-1981368341
BISAC: Cooking/Courses & Dishes/Bread
Library of Congress Control Number: 2017919175
CreateSpace Independent Publishing Platform, North Charleston, SC

All rights reserved. No part of this book may be reproduced in any form, except brief excerpts for the purpose of review, without the written permission of the Authors.

Limit of Liability/Disclaimer of Warranty; While the publisher and authors have used their best efforts in preparing this book, they make no representations or warranties with respect to the accuracy of completeness of the contents of this book and specifically disclaim any implied warranties of merchantability or fitness for a particular purpose. No warranty may be created or extended by sales representative or written sales materials. Any advice, strategies and recommendations herein may not be suitable for your situation. You should consult with a professional where appropriate. Neither the publisher nor author shall be liable for any loss of profit or any other personal or commercial damages, including but not limited to special, incidental, consequential, or other damages.

DEDICATION

This book is dedicated to our mothers, Mary & Doris, and to all who lost their battle with cancer. Our love and gratitude for what they did in shaping our lives continues beyond their death and we hope and pray that our efforts to "pay it forward," will contribute to a better life for others.

We all are born and one day we all die. But we see death by cancer as being a terrible process of physical and emotional torture, of the victims and their loved ones. Helpless, powerless, or suffering can't even begin to describe what is experienced.

With cancer, physical and emotional pain is part of the torture, but they are often outweighed by the positives that are lost. And these losses are experienced by the victim and all around them, creating an individual hell for everyone. Cancer, like the physical deterioration it causes, slowly destroys and eliminates peace; confidence; tranquility; satisfaction; mobility; dexterity, and the list goes on, but for most, it is the loss of dignity that is the most devastating of all. We do our best to help the victim maintain a semblance of dignity, but every day cancer takes a bit more, and soon even our dignity suffers.

There is nothing positive about cancer, but there are many positives of our humanity. Thankfully, when most experience pain, ours and that of others, we become mobilized to eliminate it and attempt to prevent its return. So it is with the shared pain of cancer.

There are many dedicated men and women in countless fields of endeavor that are working for a cure of this death by torture. There are also many who engage the battle by raising awareness and money to help find a cure. Today, Tina and I, together with our readers, are upping our effort of cancer awareness and contribution.

One day, all forms of cancer will be conquered, but until that day, our efforts will never falter.

Our Commitment: Ten percent of all net royalties received from the sales of this book will be donated to cancer research.

Table of Contents	Page
Acknowledgements	ix
Foreword	xi
Introduction	1
Our Daily Breads	13
English Muffin Bread: *69.1% Hydration*	14
Farmhouse Loaf: *55.0% Hydration*	18
Ms Georgia's White Bread: *55.5% Hydration*	21
Rye With Caraway: *51.88% Hydration*	24
100% Whole-Wheat: *66.32% Hydration*	27
Flatbreads	31
Detente Fougasse: *56.7% Hydration*	32
Garlic Naan: *61.43% Hydration*	35
Moroccan KESRA: *53.75% Hydration*	38
Herb Focaccia: *62.96% Hydration*	41
Pizza: *58.59% Hydration*	44
French	47
Baguette Basic & Pure: *65.0% Hydration*	48
Brioche: *66.98% Hydration*	51
Pain Ordinaire: *60.0% Hydration*	54
German	57
Pumpernickel Raisin Walnut Bread: *60.0% Hydration*	58
Rye Bread: Lynne's Grandmother: *63.0% Hydration*	62
Holiday	67
Cranberry Orange Nut Bread: *72.0% Hydration*	68
Hot Cross Buns: *67.28% Hydration*	72
Panettone Loaf: *67.82% Hydration*	75
Christmas Stollen: *61.85% Hydration*	79
Italian	83
Calzone: *56.6% Hydration*	84
Classic Italian Loaf: *60.48% Hydration*	88
Muffuletta Bread: *56.0% Hydration*	91
Muffuletta Sandwich	93
Sausage Bread: *65.0% Hydration*	97
Stromboli: *56.6% Hydration*	101
Rolls	105
Butter Rolls: *55.67% Hydration*	106
Kaiser Rolls: *58.06% Hydration*	109
Norm's New York Onion Rolls: *54.0% Hydration*	113
Onion Buns: *57.75% Hydration*	117
Parker House Rolls: *65.6% Hydration*	121
Pumpernickel Raisin Rolls: *60.0% Hydration*	125
TJ's Extra Special Crescent Rolls: *56.42% Hydration*	129
Appendix One: Cuisinart CBK-200 Cycles & Times	133

Acknowledgements

It is very clear that without the help of many friends and family, our goal to publish wouldn't have become a reality. To each of you who helped, you have our deepest gratitude.

To our mothers, aunts and grandmothers who helped us to understand, appreciate and develop skills in cooking, and baking, so important in the "Food Chain" of life and living.

To our oldest daughter, Nicole and our son-in-law Bill for the gift of a bread machine that stimulated me to begin our current bread journey.

To the "one and only" Aunt Jackie LaRosa.

To Lynne *Chudomelka* Clemens, whose friendship, food knowledge, training, and expertise provided invaluable reviews, comments and editing.

To special friends, John & Dominique Spivey and John, Nancy, and Thomas Roach.

To the best of neighbors: Peter Clemens; the Dynamic Duo of Brian McGowan & Denise Tayloe; Lisa & Mike Lewis; and to our newest neighbors and "tasters," Terri & Jeff Marantette.

To our Special Beta Tasters:
Aquia Harbor's Tuesday Morning Bridge Group who tirelessly tasted our breads and provided invaluable feedback. Anne A., Dave A., Eleanor B., Teresa B., Gladys C., Dennis C., Ken C., Bobby H., Chris H., Terry K., Sandi M., Joanie M., Clair M., Kay P., Barbara R., Grace R., Judie R., Jim S., Bonnie T., Cynthia W., John W., Madeline W.

And a special thanks to all the bakers/authors/researchers who brought us back to quality bread. I must add, that I found many print and Internet resources invaluable, but it was the format of forums/blogs that I found was a bit more satisfying. You get to explore a topic with so many points of views, and various levels of knowledge and expertise, over a period that can span years.

Together, you all have helped us to create and share our efforts with others.

x Delicious Direct Breads

Acknowledgements

It is very clear that without the help of many friends and family, our goal to publish wouldn't have become a reality. We never would have finished our efforts. To each of you who helped, you have our deepest gratitude.

To our mothers, aunts and grandmothers who helped us to understand, appreciate and develop skills in cooking, and baking, so important in the "Food Chain" of life and living.

To our oldest daughter, Nicole and our son-in-law Bill for the gift of a bread machine that stimulated me to begin our current bread journey.

To the "one and only" Aunt Jackie LaRosa.

To Lynne *Chudomelka* Clemens, whose friendship, food knowledge, training, and expertise provided invaluable reviews, comments and editing.

To special friends, John & Dominique Spivey and John, Nancy, and Thomas Roach.

To the best of neighbors: Peter Clemens; the Dynamic Duo of Brian McGowan & Denise Tayloe; Lisa & Mike Lewis; and to our newest neighbors and "tasters," Terri & Jeff Marantette.

To our Special Beta Tasters:
Aquia Harbor's Tuesday Morning Bridge Group who tirelessly tasted our breads and provided invaluable feedback. Anne A., Dave A., Eleanor B., Teresa B., Gladys C., Dennis C., Ken C., Bobby H., Chris H., Terry K., Sandi M., Joanie M., Clair M., Kay P., Barbara R., Grace R., Judie R., Jim S., Bonnie T., Cynthia W., John W., Madeline W.

And a special thanks to all the bakers/authors/researchers who brought us back to quality bread.

Together, you all have helped to create and share our efforts with others.

x Delicious Direct Breads

Foreword

A Bold Claim

Our books will save you hundreds of hours of research, and they will help to reduce the need for medication as you attempt to understand *direct* & *indirect* bread making. Save in doctor's fees, medicine and therapy. Forget anti-anxiety and anti-depressant prescriptions, and those time consuming, complicated insurance forms.

Keep *Bread Defined, Mastering Sourdough*, and *Delicious Direct Breads* by you while reading "how to" bread books of all kinds, and you will become the positive, confident, knowledgeable person sought after on bread forums. No more feelings of being an "incompetent," "stupid" person, or being a "lost soul" who is doomed to an eternity of never understanding the bread making process. No more having to buy those wonderful breads at a bakery, while the daydreamer in you escapes to a world where your bread creations rival the best of the bread masters.

Don't daydream! Gain the *confidence* that comes from *clarity, comprehension and competence*. Think ahead to a time where you will no longer be a slave to the bakery. You will be able to create great bread because you will come to understand the processes. Processes that so many times you thought you finally understood, only to have the "rug pulled out from beneath your feet," as another term or phrase meant to clarify, actually creates more confusion.

Bread Defined is different. It is more than a glossary, but it is not a "how to do" book as are *Mastering Sourdough* and *Delicious Direct Breads*. We wanted to create a "how to understand" book that serves the needs of those wanting to make good bread and enjoy themselves while doing it.

Our "how to" companion books, *Mastering Sourdough* and *Delicious Direct Breads* utilize definitions, elaborations, processes, step-by-step procedures, tables and presentation formats that provide the *clarity necessary to maximize confidence, comprehension and competence.*

If you use our trio of companion bread books, your experiences will be those of joy, happiness and enlightenment. *Your bread journey will be free of medicine & therapy!*

OK. It's a bit over the top. But seriously, we want to help make your bread experience a pleasant and rewarding one. A clearer understanding of the terms, processes and procedures involved across the minefield of *direct* and *indirect* breads will help to avoid the confusion and frustration that is often lurking behind the next bread term/process/procedure.

Our Journey

Several years ago our oldest daughter Nicole, and our son-in-law Bill gave me a bread machine and to be truthful, I don't recall why they chose that as a gift for me. She knew I liked to make bread now and then, and of course, homemade pizza was a great treat. But a bread machine?

I started reading the directions and the recipes included with the machine, and within a short time I was making fresh bread, and it was pretty good. With increasing success with different recipes, we kept expanding our efforts to include more types of breads, and this led to an increased awareness of the wide-ranging possibilities available. Learning more about the potential of our bread machine led to preparing the dough using the dough setting of the machine. For me it was great. I had always enjoyed making dough by hand, but with a bit of arthritis, kneading was not fun, and the bread machine became a wonderful partner. The fact there was also less mess and it is easier to use, made our relationship even stronger. I was now onto a path of wanting to learn more and more about bread.

We began modifying some recipes, which led us into the world of Bakers' Percentages, and the conversion of volume measurements into weight equivalents. We chose the *Metric* system over *Imperial*[1] because of its ease of use mathematically in comparison to ounces and pounds. As to temperature, we elected to provide both *Fahrenheit* and *Celsius* values.

Over time, to help with recipe presentations and modifications, we developed our recipe/formula table format and increased the type size and line spacing to enhance readability. We saw a need and developed our "Pantry of Ingredient Weights Table." This table, together with our growing "glossary," helped us to understand existing recipes and develop the ability to modify them. Why were particular ingredients used, and how much should be used? What are the metric equivalents of volume measurements?

Going beyond just following directions, resulted in being exposed to, and seeking increased understanding about different types/processes of making bread. Delving more into the history of bread led to more clarity about *direct* and *indirect* bread differences. In fact the bread making I had been familiar with was, in the course of history, a new development. Before the advent/creation of commercial yeast, all breads were prefermented breads, or *indirect* breads. But let me divert for a moment and introduce this difference.

> With *direct* bread making you are completing the process in one stage of preparation and baking, and it is the use of commercial yeast that makes this possible. This yeast is inexpensive, easy to obtain and use. It works the same around the world. It's uncomplicated, helping the understanding of *direct* bread to be uncomplicated. You essentially get bread out of the oven the same day you prepared the dough. *Indirect* bread requires the use of a portion of the recipe's total flour and water to create a pre-ferment that is later added to the rest of the flour, water and other ingredients. It often employs long and multiple rise times overnight or for several days.

---

[1] Actually, the United States customary units system of measurement.

Up to this point, we had a fair understanding and some skill development in making bread, but we were still beginners, and we were working on one book; *Pleasure Independence & Bread*. Until then, we had yet to experience the existence of pre-ferments, and were essentially ignorant of any bread making that went beyond our dealing with commercial yeast. But our world quickly expanded with our seeking to understand pre-fermented bread.

Tina joined me in my experimentation with sourdough, but gaining the knowledge was not as easy as we thought it would be. While I continued to work and write on *direct* breads, I also took on the role of researcher. I looked over the bread books available, especially those dedicated to sourdough, but I found a mixed bag of information. There were growing numbers of artisan books, and in reviewing them I saw that I had much to learn.

As the bread journey progressed deeper into *indirect* bread, I only had minor difficulties with following and understanding *sponge* formulas using *Biga* and *Poolish* pre-ferments, which use commercial yeast. However, when I investigated how to create a sourdough starter, confusion reigned. What I first thought would be a logical and fairly straight forward process of learning, turned out to be something that kept taking more and more time. The more I read about artisan bread or pre-ferments, the more I became confused. Terms, labels, and processes were either inadequately described, or in many cases improperly used. *Who to believe? Who to ignore?*

Sourdoughland

One bright and sunny day, without a care in the world, we decided to try our hand at making sourdough bread. We had been making some wonderful *Direct* breads, by our bread machine, stand mixer and food processor, but they were essentially basic, and easy to do. With commercial yeast and fairly clear directions, success with breads was achieved, and this led us to expand our horizons.

With excitement that comes from anticipation, we began searching for basic recipes and "how to" guides and books on *sourdough* and other *Indirect* breads. It was *sourdough* that brought us to the many blogs, and forums on the Internet. It was also *sourdough* that highlighted we knew much less than what we thought about bread making.

However, in spite of positive anticipation, our introduction and entry into the world of *Sourdough* was like Alice falling through the "rabbit hole" into her *Wonderland* where logic and understanding could never quite be reached.

When we found ourselves in *Sourdoughland*, it was immediately clear that you had to be very careful what you said, because each word had so many meanings that it was impossible to predict how someone would respond to what was being said. What did they really mean? All the artisans we encountered were helpful and truly eager for us to join with them in *Sourdoughland*, but it seemed impossible to reconcile what was being said about the same process or procedure by different people.

Achieving citizenship in *Sourdoughland* begins with the creation of a "starter," which some also call a "mother," "chef," "seed culture," or "levain." And in the process of creating your *starter/mother/chef/seed culture/levain* you are *emphatically* told you *must* use organic flour or that it *must* be rye flour or that it can be *any* bread flour you want.

Sourdoughland Gurus also educate how the water must be distilled, bottled, boiled or just go ahead and use tap water. Just be sure there is no chlorine. In an uncharacteristic *Sourdoughland* moment, it was uniformly agreed that your swimming pool should not be the source of the water. However, there was a voice from the back of group that claimed research is ongoing in this area.

You are reminded by the residents of *Sourdoughland*, that your *starter/chef/seed culture/levain* is a living organism, and as such it must be treated with respect and understanding. Many residents show this respect by having pet names for their *starter/mother/chef/seed culture/levain*. But, sadly, you can't name something you haven't yet created.

The creation formula and procedure seems simple enough. Begin with adding some water (bottled, boiled or just plain tap water) with some flour (organic white, rye, or just plain bread flour) and repeating this for several days, with "several" ranging from *4 or 5* to *14* days "at least." Some say to use crushed grapes in the mix as there is an abundance of wild yeast on their skins, but if not available, use raisins (once mighty grapes) soaked in warm water to bring out the yeast and sugars. It sounded rational, but others pointed out that this was nonsense, and it should be ignored. In any case, soon (non-specific; just trust it will happen) bubbles will begin and you will have created a wild yeast *starter/mother/chef/seed culture/levain* that can rise bread. After all of this, doesn't it make you wonder why not just begin with *self-rising* flour in the first place? But before we can examine this possibility, the warnings begin.

There are bad bacteria in the world, and if they get mixed in with the good bacteria they may take over and kill your *starter/mother/chef/seed culture/levain* before she/he/it gets started (Did I just make a pun? Before the *starter* can get *started*?). To prevent this tragedy, you can add pineapple juice or grapes (again with the grapes) and this will kill any bad bacteria. How and why is not understood by many, but again, just trust that it will work. On the other hand other residents of *Sourdoughland* again say to ignore this folklore, and nonsense. And while others could offer no reason, they simply insist, why take any chances, *Just Do It!* These individuals had been successful in creating their *starter/mother/chef/seed culture/levain* by using a mix of organic and non-organic wheat and rye flours, mixing with bottle, boiled and tap water at each scheduled feeding/refreshment, which varied from once to twice to three times a day with some insisting not to over-feed and they only feed every other day.

Welcome to *Sourdoughland*!

Some may feel that *Sourdoughland* is an over-exaggeration of sourdough literature, however, I am sure many have experienced similar inconsistencies and frustrations.

For me, it is clear. If I never entered *Sourdoughland*, I never would have come to fully understand and appreciate wonderful breads. The problems we encountered with *indirect* breads, resulted in our paying greater attention to *direct* breads, which in turn, helped to better understand basic bread processes. This enhanced understanding led us to make *direct* & *indirect* recipe/formula format and presentation improvements, along with the creation of a bread reference that included *Terms, Tips & Troubleshooting*.

As A Result
Taking into account our experiences to date, we decided to do several things.

- We would continue to *write down* each term we ran across so as to know and better understand what it really meant.
- We would pick procedures that seemed to provide the best and most reasonable explanation of *why* to do it their way.
- We would ensure that full and complete information necessary and helpful to the replication of each formula is provided.
- We would refine our *formula table format* to help the reader get and hold an image of the process. *Clarity* was further enhanced with the presentation of *Baker's Percentages*, *metric weights* and our *Action Table*.
- We stopped our work on *Pleasure, Independence & Bread* as it was now obvious that we had to become more focused on increasing our understanding of all kinds of bread making.

We were now on a path to write and publish three books, and the following is a brief introduction to each.

(1) Reference: *Bread Defined: Terms, Tips & Troubleshooting*. The initial process of creating a list of relevant terms expanded into a glossary and then into a reference guide including bread related terms, tips and troubleshooting. A number of the terms have elaborations that range from simple and concise all the way to expansive and wordy. In our selection and elaboration of terms we have included key ingredients used in all kinds of breads, and in many instances we provide the why and how they are used. Oh, I know it is possible to make a loaf of bread or a batch of rolls without understanding *anything* (I'm sure you know someone who is a perfect example of this), but the "tweaking" that is often needed to make a *good* formula *great*, or the recognizing and correcting of *recipe errors* requires understanding of ingredients, processes and the development of some basic skills.

(2) Pre-ferments & Sourdough "How To:" *Mastering Sourdough: Trapping, Taming & Training Wild Yeast.* Our journey into pre-ferments evolved through the research and experimentation with all types of pre-ferments. It was initially very confusing and painful, but soon, with the help of *Bread Defined*, it became enlightening and very rewarding. We take the reader through the basics of *direct* and *indirect* breads and progress to a point of true understanding and skill development with sourdough breads. You are shown how to create a starter (*Trap*), and stabilize (*Tame*) and bring it to a flexible maturity (*Train*) including, but not limited to, topics such as: *hydration, baker's percentages, refreshment schedules, starter to dough ratios, manipulating "sourness,"* and *sourdough storage*. The recipes range from those enhancing *direct* bread making to those using *mother* directly and end with creating and using *levains* through the elaboration of *mother*.

(3) Enhanced Direct Bread Formulas: *Delicious Direct Breads: Tempting, Tender & Tasty.* Our return to *direct* breads led us to a focus on increasing *clarity* in the preparation of breads. Select your bread from thirty one formulas in the categories of: *Our Daily Breads, Flatbreads, French, German, Holiday, Italian, and Rolls*. Proceed with confidence using our unique ingredient and activity tables, and an overall presentation format that utilizes easy to read type size and style.

****

All formulas created, revised and adapted have been tested using the bread machine to develop the dough. We have also evaluated mixing and kneading by hand, stand mixer, food processor, stretch & fold, and slap & fold, and other variations. Knowledge of these methods will allow you to determine your method of choice. For many reasons outlined in our books, we prefer the bread machine, even though arguments are made that you need techniques other than traditional mechanical methods of kneading to get "true artisan" breads.

You will also see methods and procedures in our books that we utilize to increase the quality of our bread, such as autolyse, long and multiple fermentation, retardation, simulating hearth baking (steam in the oven, etc) to name a few. Our goal is to help *clarify the process of bread making and baking*, and not to promote a particular method or technique over an another. It is for you, when you develop knowledge about what is available and how it works, to choose your particular path to great bread.

All three books are all scheduled to be published at the same time, and this *Foreword* is our presentation of each of them to you. *Comments & Suggestions are welcome at sergedoucette@gmail.com.* We cannot guarantee that your emails will receive a personal response, however all will be gratefully received, read, and sincerely considered.

Tina & Mickey
Stafford, Virginia
February, 2018

*I*ntroduction

Dough Preparation Methods

We have experimented with the use of four different methods of bread making in the development of our bread formulas: (1) The historically traditional "By Hand," and (2) the *20th* century "By Stand Mixer," (3) the more recent innovation, "By Bread Machine," and (4) the "Food Processor." However, it is the use of the bread machine that was used in the final completion and testing of all our formulas. Our concentration is on the formula itself, its Ingredients and Baker's Percentage Table, Action Table, and the overall format of its presentation.

Ease of reading, and step-by-step presentations that lead to a non-complicated and consistent replication of each formula is our main goal. With this in mind, it is fitting to quote from our companion book, *Mastering Sourdough*.[2]

Our focus is on clarity and not prose, although we feel a well written and well presented formula is Bread Poetry at its best.

---

[2] Serge Doucette and Bettina Doucette, *Mastering Sourdough: Trapping, Taming & Training Wild Yeast* (Self Published. Printed by CreateSpace, Charleston, 2018), 6.

Welcome to Tina's Kitchen Bakery (TKB)

We believe that you will find our bread book to be a bit different from others, and hopefully you will find that these differences are positive. The following features provide a good overview as to the reasons we believe that you will enjoy using our book, but the ultimate enjoyment of course will be eating and sharing the wonderful bread and rolls you will create.

Features

Plain English
Clear & Concise Use Of Terms
Dough Preparation
Our Bread Machine Choice
Presentation/Format
Large Type and Spacing
Formulas
Volume; Metric Weights & Percentages
Hydration
Table Format
Enhancement Procedures
Dough Development
Hearth Baking

Plain English
Clear & Concise Use of Terms

As we presented in the *Foreword*, our initial difficulties often centered around confusion with terms and process, as this led to the development of *Bread Defined, Terms, Tips & Troubleshooting*.[3] It has become a source of the improvement of our writings and presentations.

Ease of reading, and step-by-step presentations that lead to a non-complicated and consistent replication of each formula is our main goal. With this in mind, it is fitting to quote from our companion book, *Mastering Sourdough*.[4]

Our focus is on clarity and not prose, although we feel a well written and well presented formula is Bread Poetry at its best.

Dough Preparation

Whatever the method chosen, we need to pay attention to external influences, such as temperature, humidity and altitude have on the development of the dough. Also we know that different flours have different water/liquid absorption capacities, and different formulas have

---

[3] Doucette, Serge and Bettina Doucette. *Bread Defined: Terms, Tips & Troubleshooting.* Self Published. Printed by CreateSpace, Charleston, 2018.

[4] Serge Doucette and Bettina Doucette, *Mastering Sourdough: Trapping, Taming & Training Wild Yeast* (Self Published. Printed by CreateSpace, Charleston, 2018), 7.

various desired hydration levels to create a particular bread product. Low and high levels of hydration present doughs that are quite different from those in the range of *56%* to *68%*. Of course we must also be aware of and tend to dough temperature as we develop the dough.

In all methods of dough preparation a central goal is to properly develop the gluten during all stages of multiple fermentations and final proofing of the shaped dough. The *Membrane Test* assures that we have kneaded the dough enough and the gluten is properly developed. The *Poke Test* is simple to perform, and will help to prevent any chance of "under-proofing," or "over-proofing."[5] Many prefer "By Hand" methods, having developed the skill of "feeling" the proper level of moisture, temperature, texture, and the right amount of dough *extensibility* and *elasticity*,[6] while also paying attention to the dough's appearance. In using a stand mixer we initially rely on appearance, and later on the "feel" of the dough as we progress through the mixing, kneading and handling of the dough. Kneading by hand takes longer than the stand mixer, but with the stand mixer we must be careful not to over knead and overheat the dough.

Our Bread Machine Choice

Our target group isn't interested in equipping an artisan bakery in their home, but they do want the ability to make and bake great bread. A bread machine is convenient, simple to use; reduces and contains the "mess," and it eliminates virtually all the kneading. I realize that for many, the handling of the dough is an important component of their bread making experience and joy. But there are also many who either don't have the patience and skills to do it all by hand, or don't have the desire for all the mixing and kneading, or like myself, there are those where arthritis is aggravated by heavy mixing and kneading. This leaves me with the choices of the bread machine, stand mixer and food processor[7]. I personally prefer the bread machine as much less cleanup is required, and it requires the least attention when mixing and kneading.

Presentation/Format

In the development of our book we have taken feedback from our Beta Testers/Tasters and reported on their results and comments in different sections and formulas. Some Beta Testers/Tasters were quite knowledgeable about baking, while others were novices. Whatever their experiences were, we believe that their input helped to lead to a better understanding and more pleasure in baking bread.

Large Type & Spacing

The *12* point type used in the text, and the *14* point type used in the formulas results in an easy to read and follow presentation of formula text and ingredient tables. You can truly use this book "on site" to prepare the breads in this book. *You won't have to copy them.* This enhanced

---

[5] The *Membrane Test*, and *Poke Test* are described on page 10.
[6] *Extensibility*, and *elasticity* defined on page 10.
[7] Although I have read about and watched videos on *S&F* (Slap & Fold or Stretch & Fold) I found that they usually take more overall time and active action than our bread machine. However, it appears and is reported that S&F result in a more open crumb than what is achieved by other methods. It too has the advantage of being simple and easy on the hands, and many feel the "mess" is worth it. I expect that I will be experimenting with *S&F* in the near future.

format allows for normal reading (without a magnifying glass) and makes it easier to go back and forth between your work and the formula. There are many good bread books out there, but few are easy to read and use when actually doing the bread preparation.

Formulas
Volume; Metric Weights & Percentages

Our formula presentations are in keeping with a growing trend where both volume and weight measurements are given for each formula. For reasons which will become clear, we use the metric system of weight measurements. However, unlike most, we also provide the *Baker's Percentages* for each formula. This allows for greater understanding and facilitating any upsizing, downsizing or otherwise changing the formula while maintaining its integrity.

Many of you may not be interested in the *Baker's Percentage* at this time, but they have been the basis for the formation and revision of the formulas in this book. If you are new to the using of ingredients by weight, you will come to learn to use a kitchen scale and be more accurate and consistent in your baking. *Baking is a Science, and using weights and not volume makes baking much easier, more accurate, and more enjoyable.* The *Tare* function of the scale allows you to "zero out the scale," measure another ingredient, and again you "zero out the scale," and all this allows easy adding and mixing in one bowl. I presented this "argument" in *Bread Defined*.[8]

> As an example, consider the situation where we want *16* ounces, or *453.6* grams of unbleached white bread flour. In volume measurement, one cup of flour = *120g*, so we will need *3* cups (*360g*) plus *93.6g* (*453.6g - 360g = 93.6g*). *3/4* cup = *90g*, so we need *3.6g* more than *3/4* of a cup. One teaspoon of flour is equal to *2.5g* leaving *1.1g* still needed. *1.1g/2.5g = .44* or about *1/2* tsp. But *1/2* tsp actually equals *1.8* grams so we will be "slightly off." But many feel this is close enough.

> To get *453.6g* of flour you need *3 3/4*(cups) plus *1 1/2* tsp in volume measurements. In using volume you have to measure **six** times; *one* cup *3* times, *3/4* cup *1* time; *1* tsp *1* time; and *1/2* tsp *1* time, and each one of the measurements can be a source of error. *When we use weights, be it ounces or grams, we only have to weigh once.*

> We have two inexpensive scales with one being accurate to the nearest gram, and the other being accurate to *1/10* gram.[9] The more accurate one is for smaller weights and it doesn't have anywhere near the weight capacity of the other.

We use the metric system of gram/kilogram for the greatest of ease in weight measurements and conversions, and every effort has been made to ensure accuracy in our conversions from metric weights to volume and volume to metric weights.

---

[8] Doucette and Doucette, *Bread Defined*, 6.
[9] Oxyo Good Grips 11 Pound Stainless Scale; $44.99 on amazon.com and Smart Weigh ZIP 600 gram pocket scale; $13.99 on amazon.com at time of this writing.

We introduced our table and presentation format with the publication of *Mastering Sourdough*[10] and we believe that our unique presentations allow for more clarity, understanding and ease throughout the process of creating wonderful bread. When using our formula format, there is no doubt what is required.

Each of our formulas is presented in a uniform format for ease of use and consistency. In each you have an elaboration in braces, a Contributor/Source of the formula (if any); an "*Ingredient Table*" showing volume and gram weights as well as *Baker's Percentages*.

Hydration

Below each table is the Hydration (water/liquid content) of the formula. This is calculated by dividing the total liquid weight in the formula by the total flour weight, which in this case is equal to *.691* or *69.1%*. Rarely do recipe/formula authors present the Hydration values or the percentages of each of the ingredients. If you are not familiar with the reasons why hydration is so important, take the time to research on the Internet, or print references, or you can review our companion book, *Bread Defined*.[11]

Ingredient Inclusion & Exclusion In Hydration[12]

The decision of whether or not to include an ingredient into the bread product's *Hydration* is simply made by the significance of its amount of water. Obviously, ingredients without any percentage of water, such as oils, and molasses (essentially all sugar) are never included. However, there are ingredients that do contain some percentage of water, but their contribution is often considered to not be significant. In this category are honey (about *20%*), maple syrup (about *30%*), and butter (about *20%*), so together with oils and molasses, they are not included in our *Hydration* calculations. There are also ingredients that although they don't contain near *100%* water, in *Hydration* calculations they are often treated as all water. It is considered close enough for most uses. These include: fresh fruits, fruit juices, fruit purees, vinegar, milk, butter milk, cream, yogurt, and similar dairy products. We also include, as many do, whole eggs, egg whites, and egg yolks. The individual ingredient weights are taken as being *100%* water and added to the bread product's *Hydration* calculation. We adopt the position held by many that any distortion of hydration in these cases will be minimal and have essentially no impact. *See Baker's Percentage; Flour; Water.*

In each table, we provide two total flour amounts per formula allowing for the preparation of different sizes, or number of loaves/rolls. We limit total flour to *800g* and any amount over *600g* requires dough to be removed from machine and placed in a bowl to rise.

---

[10] Doucette, Serge and Bettina Doucette. *Mastering Sourdough: Trapping, Taming & Training Wild Yeast.* Self Published. Printed by CreateSpace, Charleston, 2018.
[11] Doucette and Doucette, *Bread Defined*. 2018.
[12] Doucette and Doucette, *Bread Defined*. 2018, 74.

Table Format

English Muffin Bread

Bread Machine		
A	P	Action
5		Preparation
15		Assemble & Weigh
0	100	Dough Prep
	---	1st Rise
20		Shaping
	60	Final Rise
5	40	Bake
5	30	Cool
50	230	TOTAL
0:50	3:50	4 hrs 40 min

{ This bread is great for toasting. It is flavorful with a perfect textured open crumb and it has earned "Our Favorite" in its category. Try it with the optional raisins and you won't be disappointed. }

Inspired By Several King Arthur Recipes.[13]

%	Ingredient	Volume	Grams	Volume	Grams
			400.0		800.0
13.0	Water	3Tb+2tsp	52.0	1/3C+2Tb	104.0
55.0	Milk	3/4C+2Tb+2tsp	220.0	1C+2Tb	440.0
1.1	White Vinegar	1tsp	4.4	2tsp	8.8
6.5	Melted Butter	1Tb+2 1/2tsp	26.0	3Tb+2tsp	52.0
2.06	Salt	1tsp+1/3tsp	8.25	2tsp+3/4tsp	16.5
1.38	Granulated sugar	1 1/4tsp	5.5	2tsp+3/4tsp	11.0
100.0	Unbleached bread flour	3C+1/3C	400.0	6C+2/3C	800.0
0.56	Baking powder	3/4tsp	2.25	1 1/4tsp	4.5
1.63	Rapid rise yeast	2tsp	6.5	1Tb+1tsp	13.0
22.75	Raisins; loosely packed; *Optional*	2/3C	91.0	1C+2tsp	182.0
203.98	TOTAL		815.9		1631.8
	Cornmeal	For Dusting		For Dusting	

Hydration = (52g+220g+4.4g)/400g = 276.4g/400g = .691 or 69.1%

---

[13] "English Muffin Bread," *kingarthurflour.com*, Last Accessed 11/10/2017, http://search.kingarthurflour.com/search?w=english%20muffin%20bread&af=type:recipes

6 Delicious Direct Breads

This example is an excerpt from the first formula we present in the book. It's for illustration purposes and is not compete here. Now let's take a look at the following and see the benefits of our presentation and format.

Take a moment and just look at that presentation. Come on; admit it. It's a work of art! It is truly "Bread Poetry At Its Best!" Ok, so we're a bit biased, but it sure beats the way that many present their formulas.

The leftmost column of the *Formula Table* is the *Baker's Percentage* which is the percentage of that ingredient to the total flour in the formula (ex; water=*204g/300g=68%*). The *% Total* at the bottom of the table is the Bakers Total Percentage, or *Formula Percent*. And since flour is always *100%*, the *Formula Percent* will always be above *100%*. All volume measurements are an approximation of the metric weights provided in the table. In most cases they are "close enough," however if you have any problem with a formula and are using the volume measurements, switch to the metric weights to rule out potential measurement errors.

> NOTE: In the development of our formulas we limited our rounding up/down to maintain as much accuracy as was possible, within reason. You will find ingredients in our tables rounded to *1* or two decimal places. The most practical approach is to round off to nearest gram when actually preparing the dough.

The *Ingredient Totals* at the bottom are the "starting weights," and due to normal loss, the final product can range from *80-90%* of this value.

We improve formula simplicity and clarity by having all dry ingredients, except *Enhancements* (such as raisins, nuts, etc) and all liquids together. Ingredients are listed in the Table in the order used, grouped into liquids first, and the dry ingredients follow. If butter is to be used, it is melted first and then added with the liquids. So if you use the bread machine, stand mixer or do it by hand[14], you add the dry to the liquid. If using the food processor, grab the dry and put it in the machine first and then add the liquid.

Each formula table is then followed by the Hydration value. *Please note that because we are using the Baker's Percentage in our calculations, the Hydration value can be calculated from either loaf/roll size.*

Hydration = *(52g+220g+4.4g)/400g* = 276.4g/400g = .691 or 69.1%
Hydration = *(104g+440g+8.8g)/800g* = 552.8g/800g = .691 or 69.1%

---

[14] When doing mixing by Hand: Mix all the dry together; form a well in the center; then add liquid to the well and begin mixing dry into the wet.

Action Table: Bread Machine Dough Preparation has clear directions to follow, and you can refer to the Action Chart presented in the beginning to see the *Active* and *Passive* times and the *Grand Total* of all time required.

In the *Action Table*, the "A" column is for *Active Work*, and the "P" column is the *Passive Wait/Monitor* times. *You can quickly tell at a glance what your time commitments will be.*

Disclaimer

All the times presented in our Action Tables have been the result of averaging our completion of both active and passive events in the different recipes. Our times are also influenced by the arrangement of our particular kitchen and the manner in which equipment and tools are available. For example our bread machine is on our countertop, ready to be used. Our stand mixer is in a cabinet with a lift stand to remove the need to lift to the countertop. We do a considerable amount of cooking and baking and we have two ovens; a warming drawer and a microwave to assist. We have a kitchen that is designed and sized for both of us to be cooking and baking at the same time. Also, in many cases we can, because of our frequent baking, do each in less time is presented in the table. We have adjusted them by a few minutes in each method to account for less frequent familiarity and skill. We believe that our tables reflect the conditions of an average person in their particular kitchen. This is an area that we will continue to monitor and change as more feedback is available. Please note that if there is a range of times, we provide the highest of them in the table.

Bread Machine		
A	P	Action
5		Preparation
15		Assemble & Weigh
0	100	Dough Prep
	---	1st Rise
20		Shaping
	60	Final Rise
5	40	Bake
5	30	Cool
50	230	TOTAL
0:50	3:50	4 hrs 40 min

Preparation refers to getting ready for the particular method. For example getting the bread machine, stand mixer, food processor or bowls and utensils for mixing/kneading by hand. This of course is very dependent on your given home and storage situations.

Assemble & Weigh is the same for each method.

Dough Preparation is the actual time to mix and knead the dough and place for *1st* rise. In the case of the bread machine, the mixing and kneading is passive, but there are times where specific action needs to be done, such as using a spatula to aid the mixing process. Or the time it takes to add Enhancements, such as raisins, nuts, etc. *All bread machine times and procedures are specific to our Cuisinart Convection Bread Machine; CBK-200.*[15] *Your dough preparation times and procedures may vary, so be sure to check your machine against ours, and make any adjustments, if necessary.*

1st rise is self explanatory.

---

[15] Refer to Appendix One for Cuisinart CBK-200 cycles and times.

8 Delicious Direct Breads

Shaping (including any required resting) is self explanatory.

Final Rise is self explanatory.

Bake is self explanatory. We add 5 minutes of active time for "handling."

Cool is the self evident process of letting the bread finish its baking and cooling on the wire rack. However this time can be zero or a few minutes it is to be served hot or warm. In general, we add 5 minutes of active time for "handling."

Total is the total time in minutes for all the above Active and Passive times. And below that is the total time in hours and minutes, with the Grand Total time just to the right of that.

The Formula Table is then followed by clear directions, beginning with attention to "Preparation."

You will also notice that all ingredients listed outside of the Table are underlined. This makes it easy to identify ingredients as we go from reading to implementing the formula, reducing the chances of errors.

===

Preparation

- Be sure to review the recipe, and your machine's requirements before proceeding.
- Assemble and weigh/measure all ingredients. It will make your work much easier to have all weighed/measured and ready to follow directions.
- Ensure milk and water are at *85°F/29.4°C – 95°F/35°C* (can use microwave on high for about 40 seconds. Test with your particular microwave oven) and that the butter is softened/melted.
- Liquid Mix: Mix the water, milk, white vinegar, melted butter, salt, and sugar in a medium (large if mixing by Hand) bowl.
- Flour Mix: Mix baking powder with bread flour in an appropriately sized bowl.

===

Enhancement Procedures

The following features help to enhance the appearance, crust, crumb and flavors of the final product whatever dough preparation method is used.

Dough Development

Properly mix the ingredients and knead the dough. We want the ingredients incorporated, and the gluten strands developed and create a structure that will be able to hold the gases created during fermentation. This is achieved when we reach a balance of *extensibility* (ability to be stretched to new shape) and *elasticity* (ability to return to its shape after being stretched).[16]

Gluten: (1) The combination of the proteins *gliadin* and *glutenin* that results when flour is hydrated. The *glutenin* forms strands of long, thin, chainlike molecules, while the *gliadin* links the strands of glutenin together, forming the gluten network. Gluten development is defined by the *dough strength*, and provides the structure to trap and hold gases from the fermentation processes of the yeast and lactobacilli (leavening). Ingredients and how the dough is manipulated will result in a tight, dense crumb or the opposite with large open and irregular holes.

Dough Strength: (1) A balance of *elasticity* and *extensibility* in bread dough. *Gluten* forms with the addition and mixing of water with the flour, and gluten is what gives the dough these two characteristics. Weak dough is not very elastic, but it is very extensible. Strong dough is very elastic, but not very extensible. (2) This is one of the reasons many prefer to continue to knead by hand. Over time you get a "feel" for when the dough has developed the right amount of gluten. *See this section: Gluten; Dough Mixing/Kneading; Properly Developed Dough.*

> *Elasticity:* The ability of a dough to stretch and to return to its original shape. *Contrast with Extensibility.*

> *Extensibility:* The ability of a dough to stretch without tearing or springing back. *Contrast with Elasticity.*

Knowing When Gluten Is Ready: 1. *Feel & Appearance*: The dough should be smooth and slightly sticky to the touch; 2. *Maintains Shape*: Hold the dough ball in your hand. If it holds its ball shape, the gluten is strong. If it sags, the gluten is not yet fully developed. 3. *Membrane Test*: If you can slowly stretch the dough, without it tearing, till it forms a translucent membrane, the dough has been kneaded long enough to develop the gluten.

Long & multiple fermentations: Fermentation: (1) the process by which yeast metabolizes sugars to produce carbon dioxide and alcohol as byproducts. Fermentation is what causes dough to expand and develop flavor. Also, another type of fermentation occurs in sourdough breads, caused by lactobacillus organisms that flavor the finished loaves by creating lactic and acetic acids. (2) (bulk fermentation, first fermentation) the period of time the dough rests after mixing and before dividing/shaping.

Proofing Dough: We need to determine when the dough has reached its max development during each fermentation and following when it is shaped for its last rise/fermentation. *Poke Test*: Stick an index finger into the dough. If the dough springs back and the dent disappears, it is not ready. If the dent remains and does not spring back at all, it is over proofed and will not

---

[16] Definitions from: Doucette and Doucette, *Bread Defined*. 2018, 55.

rise fully. However, if the dent fills in about halfway, then the gluten is properly developed, and it is properly "proofed."

Benching: Resting fermented dough before and/or during shaping so that the gluten relaxes, making it easier to form (Improves extensibility).

Shaping Dough: We prepare the dough for bread tins as well as creating free form shapes.
    Letter Fold Shaping for rectangular shapes (such as bread tins) or a variation for baguettes; *Boule/Ball* shaping for round loaves; *Torpedo* shaping for batards.

Docking/Slashing: In most cases we dock our loaves to allow for maximum oven spring and to control how and where it expands. Also, by using different ways of *Docking* we can change the presentation of the finished loaf.

Hearth Baking

Maintain Temperature: Before you put your shaped loaf or rolls in the oven, you want to have even heat at the correct stable temperature so we preheat and have the oven at the specified temperature for at least *15* minutes before placing shaped dough into the oven. The use of a Pizza stone on the middle rack (where we normally bake) helps to maintain an even temperature, while additionally providing an excellent baking surface.

High oven temperature initially, and then turned down for remainder of baking. We do this to compensate for the heat loss resulting from opening the oven door to place the shaped dough in the oven and to add ice cubes to the preheated cast iron pan to create steam.

Moisture During Baking: There are instances, such as with artisan breads, that you want to maintain moisture (steam) in the oven during the first *10* minutes of baking. This helps to keep the crust soft and assist with maximum oven spring. This is achieved by keeping a cast iron pan on the bottom shelf coming to oven temperature during preheating. After putting the dough in the oven, we add ice cubes to the preheated cast iron pan and close the oven door promptly, creating steam. We maintain the moisture by spraying water into the oven at regular intervals. The pan of water is removed after *10* minutes to continue baking with dry heat.

Final Comments
Doneness: When Is It Ready?

Doneness is best recognized by the appearance of the bread; golden or golden brown crust, and is verified by checking with an instant read thermometer registering *195°F/90.6°C – 210°F/98.9°C*. Be sure to bake the recommended time as the internal temperature of the bread can reach these values before the bread is fully baked. This is why it is important to pay attention to the appearance of the bread first. I find that it is the rustic breads (Italian, French, etc) that are closer to the *210°F/98.9°C*, and our "regular" loaves are done at *195°F/90.6°C*, or a little higher.

How I Choose My Dough Preparation Method

- If I want the easiest, I first go for the bread machine as it often can do the *1st* rise in the machine. However due to its fast dough prep time my second choice is the food processor.

- If I want cleanest, or least "messy." I again choose the bread machine with its single mixing bowl. True, the stand mixer has one mixing bowl, but it takes a lot of care and practice not to get any flour on the counter or floor. Plus you have to scrape of the mixing paddle and dough hook. And what about the food processor? For me, it is the most difficult to clean, and everything should be dry before reassembling.

- If I want the best "artisan" loaf possible, I would likely utilize one of the variations of the "Stretch & Fold" technique. The "kid" in me is looking forward to trying this "messy" method, but the adult isn't too sure it's worth the extra time and mess. I will keep an open mind.

All in all, regardless of the method chosen, if you follow our formulas we believe you will achieve the promise of the sub-title; bread that is "*Tempting, Tender & Tasty*."

Our Daily Breads

English Muffin Bread

Bread Machine		
A	P	Action
5		Preparation
15		Assemble & Weigh
0	100	Dough Prep
	---	1st Rise
20		Shaping
	60	Final Rise
5	40	Bake
5	30	Cool
50	230	TOTAL
0:50	3:50	4 hrs 40 min

This bread is great for toasting. It is flavorful with a perfect textured open crumb and it has earned "Our Favorite" in its category. Try it with the optional raisins and you won't be disappointed.

Inspired By Several King Arthur Recipes.[17]

%	Ingredient	Volume	Grams	Volume	Grams
			400.0		**800.0**
13.0	Water	3Tb+2tsp	52.0	1/3C+2Tb	104.0
55.0	Milk	3/4C+2Tb+2tsp	220.0	1C+2Tb	440.0
1.1	White Vinegar	1tsp	4.4	2tsp	8.8
6.5	Melted Butter	1Tb+2 1/2tsp	26.0	3Tb+2tsp	52.0
2.06	Salt	1tsp+1/3tsp	8.25	2tsp+3/4tsp	16.5
1.38	Granulated sugar	1 1/4tsp	5.5	2tsp+3/4tsp	11.0
100.0	Unbleached bread flour	3C+1/3C	400.0	6C+2/3C	800.0
0.56	Baking powder	3/4tsp	2.25	1 1/4tsp	4.5
1.63	Rapid rise yeast	2tsp	6.5	1Tb+1tsp	13.0
22.75	Raisins; loosely packed; *Optional*	2/3C	91.0	1C+2tsp	182.0
203.98	**TOTAL**		**815.9**		**1631.8**
	Cornmeal	For Dusting		For Dusting	

Hydration = (104g+440g+8.8g)/800g = 552.8g/800g = .691 or 69.1%

---

[17] "English Muffin Bread," *kingarthurflour.com*, Last Accessed 11/10/2017, http://search.kingarthurflour.com/search?w=english%20muffin%20bread&af=type:recipes

14 Delicious Direct Breads

Preparation

- Be sure to review the recipe, and your machine's requirements before proceeding.
- Assemble and weigh/measure all ingredients. It will make your work much easier to have all weighed/measured and ready to follow directions.
- Ensure milk and water are at *85°F/29.4°C – 95°F/35°C* (can use microwave on high for about *40* seconds. Test with your particular microwave oven) and that the butter is softened/melted.
- Liquid Mix: Mix the water, milk, white vinegar, melted butter, salt, and sugar in a medium (large if mixing by Hand) bowl, or use the bread pan fitted with the kneading paddle if utilizing the Bread Machine.
- Flour Mix: Mix baking powder with bread flour.

Bread Machine

- Place the Liquid Mix in the bread pan fitted with kneading paddle and then cover with the Flour Mix. Make a shallow hole in the center and put in the yeast.

- Place the bread pan in the bread maker. Press *Menu* and select *Dough Cycle*. Select *1* lb (*400g* flour) or *2* lb (*800g* flour) loaf. Press *Start* to mix, knead, and rise. Total Time = *1:25* for *1* lb loaf; *1:40* for *2* lb loaf. If you are making the single loaf (*400g* flour) then the dough can remain in the machine for its rise. However, if you are making two loaves (*800g* total flour) then you **must** remove the dough after mixing/kneading is done, and place it in an oiled bowl large enough to handle the dough doubling in size.

- When mix-in signal alarms *(1 lb loaf = 1:12; 2 lb loaf = 1:19 Remaining),* add any ingredients, such as raisins, if desired.

- **For *400g* total flour**: When Cycle is complete, gently punch down dough and turn out on a floured work surface. Turn the bread machine off. ***Go To Prep & Shape.***

- **For *800g* total flour**: When mixing/kneading is done (*1:05* on timer), remove the dough from the bread pan and turn out on a floured surface. Turn the bread machine off. Remove the kneading paddle (if stuck into the dough) and shape the dough into a ball. Place in the oiled bowl (large enough to handle the doubling of the dough), and turn to coat all of the dough. Cover with plastic wrap and place in a warm place to rise for *45- 60* minutes, or until just about double in bulk.

Prep & Shape

- Lightly oil one or two *2* lb loaf pans/tins (*7 1/4" x 4 1/2"*), and coat surfaces with cornmeal. Roll the dough out so that it is the length of the bread pan, and *3* times its width. We found that it was best to let the dough rest for *10* minutes during this shaping. After rolling out, from the longer side, fold one third down, and then fold one third up. Tuck the ends in a bit and flip over with seam on the bottom. Place the dough, seam down in the oiled bread pan and push slightly to have it fill the pan, if necessary. Let rise for *45-60* minutes, or until double in bulk. Meanwhile, preheat oven to *400°F/204.4°C*.

Prep & Bake

- When dough is ready, make a long slit about *1/4"* deep lengthwise, and baste or spritz dough with <u>water</u> and *sprinkle a bit more <u>cornmeal</u> over the loaf*.

- Bake for about *40 minutes.* **After *5* minutes, reduce oven temperature to *375°F/190.6°C*.**

NOTE: I prefer to bake about *30* minutes and then remove from the oven and take the loaf out of the pan. I then put it back in the oven directly on the baking stone and finish baking.

- Remove from oven and check doneness with instant read thermometer (*195°F/90.6°C – 210°F/98.9°C*). Remove from pan and transfer to a wire rack to cool. Sufficiently cooling the Bread allows the flavors to develop and it makes it easier to slice (If I can resist temptation, after *30-60* minutes on cooling rack, I place loaf in a paper bag and put in the refrigerator to cool. This helps slicing quite a bit).

Notes

Farmhouse Loaf

{ The flour-dusted split top give a charmingly rustic look to this tasty whole wheat-enriched white loaf. You may want to experiment with adding raisins or nuts. }

Bread Machine		
A	P	Action
5		Preparation
15		Assemble & Weigh
5	100	Dough Prep
----		1st Rise
15	10	Shaping
	60	Final Rise
5	40	Bake
5	30	Cool
50	240	TOTAL
0:50	4:00	4 hrs 50 min

Farmhouse loaf: a large long piece of white bread with a curved top.[18]

%	Ingredient	Volume	Grams	Volume	Grams
			300.0		***600.0***
55.0	Water	2/3C+1Tbs	165.0	1C+1/3C+2Tbs	330.0
5.83	Butter	1tbs+1/2tsp	16.0	2Tbs+1 1/4tsp	32.0
1.75	Salt	1 tsp	5.25	1 3/4tsp	10.5
1.17	Granulated sugar	3/4tsp	3.5	1 3/4tsp	7.0
80.0	Unbleached white bread flour	2C	240.0	4C	480.0
20.0	Whole-wheat bread flour	1/2C	60.0	1C	120.0
1.33	Non-fat dry milk	2tsp	4.0	4tsp	8.0
2.50	Vital Wheat Gluten	3tsp	7.5	6tsp	15.0
0.67	Rapid rise yeast	3/4tsp	2.4	1 1/4tsp	4.8
168.25	TOTAL		496.15		992.3

Hydration = *330g/(480g+120g) = 330g/600g = .55 or 55.0%*

---

[18] From: http://www.macmillandictionary.com/dictionary/british/farmhouse-loaf

18 Delicious Direct Breads

Preparation

- Be sure to review the recipe, and your machine's requirements before proceeding.
- Assemble and weigh/measure all ingredients. It will make your work much easier to have all weighed/measured and ready to follow directions.
- Ensure water at *85°F/29.4°C – 95°F/35°C*.
- Soften/melt butter.
- Liquid Mix: Mix the water, melted butter, salt and sugar into a medium (large if mixing by Hand) bowl, or use the bread pan fitted with the kneading paddle if utilizing the Bread Machine.
- Flour Mix: Mix flours, dry milk powder, and vital wheat gluten in large bowl.

Bread Machine

- Place the Liquid Mix in the bread pan fitted with kneading paddle and then cover with the Flour Mix. Make a shallow hole in the center and put in the yeast.

- Place the bread pan in the bread maker. Press *Menu* and select *Dough Cycle*. Select *1* lb (*300g* flour) or *2* lb (*600g* flour) loaf. Press *Start* to mix, knead, and rise. Total Time = *1:25* for *1* lb loaf; *1:40* for *2* lb loaf.

- When mix in signal sounds add any additional ingredients *(1 lb loaf = 1:12; 2 lb loaf = 1:19 Remaining)*.

- When dough cycle is complete, remove and place dough on floured work surface. Turn off the machine.

Prep & Shape

- Lightly oil one or two *2* lb loaf pans/tins (*7 1/4" x 4 1/2"*). Roll the dough out so that it is the length of the bread pan, and *3* times its width. We found that it was best to let the dough rest for *10* minutes during this shaping. After rolling out, from the longer side, fold one third down, and then fold one third up. Tuck the ends in a bit and flip over with seam on the bottom. Place the dough, seam down in the oiled bread pan and push slightly to have it fill the pan, if necessary. Let rise for *45-60* minutes, or until double in bulk. Meanwhile, prepare and preheat oven to *425°F/218.3°C*.

Prep & Bake

- When dough is ready, spritz loaf with <u>water</u> and sprinkle <u>flour</u> over the loaf. Make a long slit about *1/4"* deep lengthwise.

- Bake for *15* min, then reduce the oven temperature to *400°F/204.4°C* and bake for *20-25* minutes more, or until golden.

- Remove from oven and check doneness with instant read thermometer (*195°F/90.6°C – 210°F/98.9°C)*. When done, remove from pan and transfer to a wire rack to cool.

Notes

Ms Georgia's White Bread

Bread Machine		
A	P	Action
5		Preparation
15		Assemble & Weigh
5	100	Dough Prep
	----	1st Rise
15	10	Shaping
	60	Final Rise
5	50	Bake
5	30	Cool
50	250	TOTAL
0:50	4:10	5 hrs 00 min

{ A longtime friend of Lynne's parents, Ms Georgia was born in and still lives in Elkland, Mo. about nine miles from where Lynne grew up. }

Contributors: TKB Kitchen Bakery; Ms Georgia and The Clemens Family

%	Ingredient	Volume	Grams	Volume	Grams
			360.0		**720.0**
18.0	Water; lukewarm*	1/4c+1 1/2tsp	65.0	1/2C+1Tb+1/2tsp	130.0
37.5	Milk; Lukewarm	1/2C+1Tb	135.0	1C+2Tbs	270.0
16.11	Sugar	1/4C+2 1/2tsp	58.0	1/2C+1Tb+2tsp	116.0
1.94	Salt	1 1/4 tsp	7.0	1 1/3 tsp	14.0
11.81	Butter	3 Tb	42.5	1/3C+2tsp	85.0
100.0	Unbleached white bread flour	3C	360.0	6C	720.0
1.4	Rapid Rise Yeast	1 2/3 tsp	5.06	3 1/4 tsp	10.11
186.76	TOTAL		672.56		1345.11

Hydration = (130g+270g)/720g = 400g/720g = .556 or 55.6%

* You can replace the water with milk if desired. The water was used in the original formula to dissolve the yeast.

Preparation

- Be sure to review the recipe, and your machine's requirements before proceeding.
- Assemble and weigh/measure all ingredients. It will make your work much easier to have all weighed/measured and ready to follow directions.
- Ensure <u>milk</u> and <u>water</u> at *85°F/29.4°C – 95°F/35°C*
- Soften/melt <u>butter</u>.

- <u>Liquid Mix</u>: Mix <u>water</u>, <u>milk</u>, <u>sugar</u>, <u>salt</u> and <u>melted butter</u> in a medium (large if mixing by Hand) bowl, or use the bread pan fitted with the kneading paddle if utilizing the Bread Machine.

Bread Machine

- Pour the <u>Liquid Mix</u> into the bread pan fitted with the kneading paddle and then cover with the <u>flour</u>. Make a shallow hole in the center and put in the <u>yeast</u>.

- Place the bread pan in the bread maker. Press *Menu* and select *Dough Cycle*. Select *1* lb (*360g* flour) or *2* lb (*720g* flour) loaf. Press *Start* to mix, knead, and rise. Total Time = *1:25* for *1* lb loaf; *1:40* for *2* lb loaf. You will need to assist the mixing and kneading, especially if you are preparing the *720g* of flour formula. It will initially be a gnarly and sticky mass but with assistance it will tighten up in about *15* minutes. It will eventually be supple and smooth.

- **For *360g* total flour**: When Cycle is complete, gently punch down dough and turn out on a floured work surface. Turn the bread machine off. ***Go To Prep & Shape.***

- **For *720g* total flour**: When mixing/kneading is done (*1:05* on timer), remove the dough from the bread pan and turn out on a floured surface. Turn the bread machine off. Remove the kneading paddle (if stuck into the dough) and shape the dough into a ball. Place in the oiled bowl (large enough to handle the doubling of the dough), and turn to coat all of the dough. Cover with plastic wrap and place in a warm place to rise for *45-60* minutes, or until just about double in bulk.

- When ready, gently punch down dough and turn out on a floured work surface

Prep & Shape

- Lightly oil one or two *2* lb loaf pans/tins (*7 1/4" x 4 1/2"*). Roll the dough out so that it is the length of the bread pan, and *3* times its width.

- We found that it was best to let the dough rest for *10* minutes during this shaping. After rolling out, from the longer side, fold one third down, and then fold one third up. Tuck the ends in a bit and flip over with seam on the bottom. Place the dough, seam down in the oiled bread pan and push slightly to have it fill the pan, if necessary. Let rise for *45-60* minutes, or until double in bulk. Meanwhile, preheat oven to *325°F/162.8°C*.

Prep & Bake

- When dough is ready, baste or spritz dough with <u>water</u> and make a long slit about *1/4"* deep lengthwise. Bake for *45 - 50* minutes; until brown.

- Remove from oven and check doneness with instant read thermometer (*195°F/90.6°C – 210°F/98.9°C)*. Remove from pan and transfer to a wire rack to cool.

Notes

Rye with Caraway

{ Contrast this with Lynne's Grandmother's Rye Bread in the *German* Section. }

Bread Machine		
A	P	Action
5		Preparation
15		Assemble & Weigh
10	100	Dough Prep
	----	1st Rise
15	10	Shaping
	60	Final Rise
5	40	Bake
5	30	Cool
55	240	TOTAL
0:55	4:00	4 hrs 55 min

Inspired By Bread & Bread Machines[19]

%	Ingredient	Volume	Grams	Volume	Grams
			400.0		**800.0**
50.0	Water;85-95F	3/4C+2 Tbs	200.0	1 3/4C	400.0
1.63	Salt	1 tsp	6.5	2 tsp	13.0
1.88	Lemon juice	1/2 Tbs	7.5	1 Tbs	15.0
3.75	Sunflower oil	1 Tbs	15.0	2 Tbs	30.0
2.25	Light brown sugar	1/2Tbs+1/2tsp	9.0	1Tbs+1tsp	18.0
17.5	Rye flour	2/3C	70.0	1 1/3C	140.0
82.5	Unbleached white bread flour	2 3/4C	330.0	5.5C	660.0
1.5	Non-fat dry milk	1 Tbs	6.0	2 Tbs	12.0
1.0	Caraway seeds	1.5 tsp	4.0	3 tsp	8.0
0.78	Rapid rise yeast	1 tsp	3.11	2 tsp	6.22
162.79	**TOTAL**		**651.11**		**1302.22**

Hydration = (400g+15g)/(140g+660g) = 415g/800g = .5188 or 51.88%

Preparation

- Be sure to review the recipe, and your machine's requirements before proceeding.
- Assemble and weigh/measure all ingredients. It will make your work much easier to have all weighed/measured and ready to follow directions.

---

[19] Ingram, Christine, and Jennie Shapter. *The Complete Book of Bread & Bread Machines.* London: Hermes House, 2002, 2008.

- <u>Liquid Mix</u>: Mix the <u>water</u> *(85°F/29.4°C – 95°F/35°C),* <u>salt</u>, <u>lemon juice</u>, <u>sunflower oil</u> and <u>sugar</u> in a medium (large if mixing by Hand) bowl, or use the bread pan fitted with the kneading paddle if utilizing the Bread Machine.
- <u>Flour Mix</u>: Combine <u>flours</u>, and <u>dry milk powder</u> in large bowl.

Bread Machine

- Pour the <u>Liquid Mix</u> into the bread pan fitted with the kneading paddle and then cover with the <u>Flour Mix</u>. Make a shallow hole in the center of the <u>Flour MIX</u> and put in the <u>yeast</u>.

- Place the bread pan in the bread maker. Press *Menu* and select *Dough Cycle*. Select *1* lb (*400g* flour) or *2* lb (*800g* flour) loaf. Press *Start* to mix, knead, and rise. Total Time = *1:25* for *1* lb loaf; *1:40* for *2* lb loaf. You will need to assist the mixing and kneading, especially if you are preparing the *800g* of flour formula. It will initially be a gnarly and sticky mass but with assistance it will tighten up in about *15* minutes. It will eventually be supple and smooth.

- When Mix-in's tone sounds (*1 lb loaf = 1:12; 2 lb loaf = 1:19 Remaining*), <u>add caraway seeds</u> .

- **For *400g* total flour**: When Cycle is complete, gently punch down dough and turn out on a floured work surface. Turn the bread machine off. ***Go To Prep & Shape.***

- **For *800g* total flour**: When mixing/kneading is done (*1:05* on timer), remove the dough from the bread pan and turn out on a floured surface. Turn the bread machine off. Remove the kneading paddle (if stuck into the dough) and shape the dough into a ball. Place in the oiled bowl (large enough to handle the doubling of the dough), and turn to coat all of the dough. Cover with plastic wrap and place in a warm place to rise for *45- 60* minutes, or until just about double in bulk.

- When ready, gently punch down dough and turn out on a floured work surface.

Prep & Shape

- Lightly oil one or two *2* lb loaf pans/tins (*7 1/4" x 4 1/2"*). Roll the dough out so that it is the length of the bread pan, and *3* times its width. We found that it was best to let the dough rest for *10* minutes during this shaping. After rolling out, from the longer side, fold one third down, and then fold one third up. Tuck the ends in a bit and flip over with seam on the bottom. Place the dough, seam down in the oiled bread pan and push slightly to have it fill the pan, if necessary. Let rise for *45-60* minutes, or until double in bulk. Meanwhile, prepare and preheat oven to *375°F/190.6°C* (We have used *400°F/204.4°C* and reduced oven time by about *10* minutes).

Prep & Bake

- When dough is ready, baste dough with <u>water</u> and make a long slit about *1/4"* deep lengthwise Bake for about *40* minutes.

- Remove from oven and check doneness with instant read thermometer (*195°F/90.6°C – 210°F/98.9°C)*. Remove from pan and transfer to a wire rack to cool.

Notes

100% Whole Wheat Bread

Bread Machine		
A	P	Action
5		Preparation
15		Assemble & Weigh
10	100	Dough Prep
	----	1st Rise
15	10	Shaping
	60	Final Rise
5	40	Bake
5	30	Cool
55	240	TOTAL
0:55	4:00	4 hrs 55 min

This loaf shows that whole-wheat breads can be delicious as well as being healthy for you. Not a fan of whole-wheat? Try this and be prepared to change your tastes.

Adapted from King Arthur[20]

%	Ingredient	Volume	Grams	Volume	Grams
			400.0		**800.0**
66.32	Water; lukewarm	1C+2Tb+2tsp	265.28	2 1/3 C	530.56
7.02	Extra Virgin Olive Oil	1Tb+2 2/3tsp	28.08	3Tb+2 1/4tsp	56.16
20.12	Honey	3Tb+ 2tsp	80.48	1/3C+2Tb	160.96
2.11	Salt	1 1/2 tsp	8.44	2 7/8 tsp	16.88
100.0	Whole-Wheat Flour	3 1/3 C	400.0	6 2/3 C	800.0
1.75	Vital Wheat Gluten	1 Tb	7.0	2 Tb	14.0
1.09	Rapid Rise Yeast	1 1/2 tsp	4.36	2 7/8 tsp	8.72
198.41	**TOTAL**		**793.64**		**1587.28**
	Sesame, Sunflower, and/or flax seeds	Optional		1/4 C	35.0

Hydration = *530.56g/800g = .6632 or 66.32%*

Preparation

- Be sure to review the recipe, and your machine's requirements before proceeding.
- Assemble and weigh/measure all ingredients. It will make your work much easier to have all weighed/measured and ready to follow directions.

---

[20] "100% Whole Wheat Bread For The Bread Machine," *kingarthurflour.com*, Last Accessed 11/10/2017, https://www.kingarthurflour.com/recipes/100-whole-wheat-bread-for-the-bread-machine-recipe

- Ensure <u>water</u> at *80°F/26.7°C – 90°F/32.2°C*.
- <u>Liquid Mix</u>: Mix the <u>water</u>, <u>extra virgin olive oil</u>, <u>honey</u> and <u>salt</u> into a medium (large if mixing by Hand) bowl, or use the bread pan fitted with the kneading paddle if utilizing the Bread Machine.
- <u>Flour Mix</u>: Mix <u>flour</u> and <u>vital wheat gluten</u> into an appropriately sized bowl.

Bread Machine

- Pour the <u>Liquid Mix</u> into the bread pan fitted with the kneading paddle and then cover with the <u>Flour Mix</u>. Make a shallow hole in the center and put in the <u>yeast</u>.

- Place the bread pan in the bread maker. Press *Menu* and select *Dough Cycle*. Select *1* lb (*400g* flour) or *2* lb (*800g* flour) loaf. Press *Start* to mix, knead, and rise. Total Time = *1:25* for *1* lb loaf; *1:40* for *2* lb loaf. You will need to assist the mixing and kneading, especially if you are preparing the *800g* of flour formula. It will initially be a gnarly and sticky mass but with assistance it will tighten up in about *15* minutes. It will eventually become supple and smooth.

- **For *400g* total flour**: When Cycle is complete, gently punch down dough and turn out on a floured work surface. Turn the bread machine off. ***Go To Prep & Shape.***

- **For *800g* total flour**: When mixing/kneading is done (*1:05* on timer), remove the dough from the bread pan and turn out on a floured surface. Turn the bread machine off. Remove the kneading paddle (if stuck into the dough) and shape the dough into a ball. Place in the oiled bowl (large enough to handle the doubling of the dough), and turn to coat all of the dough. Cover with plastic wrap and place in a warm place to rise for *45-60* minutes, or until just about double in bulk.

- When ready, gently punch down dough and turn out on a floured work surface.

Prep & Shape

- Lightly oil one or two *2* lb loaf pans/tins (*7 1/4" x 4 1/2"*). Roll the dough out so that it is the length of the bread pan, and *3* times its width. We found that it was best to let the dough rest for *10* minutes during this shaping. After rolling out, from the longer side, fold one third down, and then fold one third up. Tuck the ends in a bit and flip over with seam on the bottom. Place the dough, seam down in the oiled bread pan and push slightly to have it fill the pan, if necessary. Let rise for *60 - 90* minutes, or until double in bulk. Meanwhile, prepare and preheat oven to *375°F/190.6°C*.

Bake

- Bake at *375°F/190.6°C* for about *35* minutes.

- Remove from oven and check doneness with instant read thermometer (*195°F/90.6°C – 200°F/93.33°C)*. Remove from pan and transfer to a wire rack to cool.

Notes

30 Delicious Direct Breads

*F*latbreads

Detente Fougasse

Bread Machine		
A	P	Action
5		Preparation
15		Assemble & Weigh
5	100	Dough Prep
	----	1st Rise
20	10	Shaping
	45	Final Rise
5	25	Bake
5	30	Cool
55	210	TOTAL
0:55	3:30	4 hrs 25 min

Pronounced: dey-**tahnt** *Foo-**Gahss*** *French* Greet *Greeks* in this flavorful combination of a classic French Bread with Greek Kalamata (Ka-la-ma-ta) Olives.

Adapted From Bread &Bread Machines[21]

%	Ingredient	Volume	Grams	Volume	Grams
			300.0		**600.0**
56.70	Water	3/4C	170.1	1 1/2C	340.2
4.0	Extra virgin olive oil	2 1/2tsp	12.0	1 Tbs+ 2tsp	24.0
1.6	Salt	3/4tsp	4.8	1 1/2tsp	9.6
1.0	Granulated sugar	1/2tsp	3.0	1tsp	6.0
100	Unbleached white bread flour	2.5C	300.0	5C	600.0
0.84	Rapid rise yeast	3/4tsp+1/8tsp	2.52	1 1/2tsp+ 1/8tsp	5.04
19.0	Pitted Black Kalamata Olives	1/4C+ 1 1/2tsp	57.0	1/2C+1Tb	114.0
183.14	TOTAL		549.42		1098.84

Hydration = *340.2g/600g = .567 or 56.7%*

Preparation
- Be sure to review the recipe, and your machine's requirements before proceeding.
- Assemble and weigh/measure all ingredients. It will make your work much easier to have all weighed/measured and ready to follow directions.

---

[21] Christine Ingram and Jennie Shapter. *The Complete Book of Bread & Bread Machines.* (London: Hermes House, 2002, 2008), 356.

32 Delicious Direct Breads

- Ensure <u>water</u> at *80°F/26.7°C – 90°F/32.2°C*.
- <u>Liquid Mix</u>: Combine <u>water</u>, <u>olive oil</u>, <u>salt</u> and <u>sugar</u> in a medium (large if mixing by Hand) bowl, or use the bread pan fitted with the kneading paddle if utilizing the Bread Machine.

Bread Machine

- Place the <u>Liquid Mix</u> in the bread pan fitted with kneading paddle and then cover with the <u>flour</u>. Make a shallow hole in the center and put in the <u>yeast</u>.

- Place the bread pan in the bread maker. Press *Menu* and select *Dough Cycle*. Select *1* lb (*300g* flour) or *2* lb (*600g* flour) loaf. Press *Start* to mix, knead, and rise. Total Time = *1:25* for *1* lb loaf; *1:40* for *2* lb loaf.

- When dough cycle is complete, remove dough and place onto a lightly greased or floured surface and gently punch down.

- If making *2* loaves (*600g* of total flour), divide the dough in half. Pat and stretch the dough into a flat rectangle about *4* inches by *8* inches and *1/2* inch thick. Sprinkle the <u>olives</u> over the dough, and fold it three or four times to encase the <u>olives</u>. Let rest ten minutes.

Prep & Shape

-Flatten the dough and pat and shape it into an oblong, about *12* inches long. Make *several* parallel diagonal slashes through the body of the dough, but leaving the edges intact. Using your fingers, gently stretch the fougasse dough at the slashes so that it looks like a ladder.

- Place the shaped dough on a parchment lined baking sheet. Cover with oiled plastic wrap and leave in a warm place until the dough has doubled in bulk; about *45* minutes. Meanwhile, prepare and preheat oven to *450°F/232.2°C*.

Prep & Bake

- When dough is ready, brush the top with <u>olive oil</u>, and bake for *20-25* minutes (If your oven doesn't heart evenly, rotate the bread halfway through baking.). **After five minutes**, turn the oven down to *425°F/218.3°C* and continue baking for the remainder of the time, or until the bread is golden brown. I look for the internal temperature to be between *195°F/90.6°C – 210°F/98.9°C*.

- Cool on a wire rack. Best taste and flavor after *30 - 60* min of cooling.

Notes

Garlic Naan

Garlic provides a wonderful flavor for this traditional Indian flatbread. I don't have any proof, but I believe it is the most favorite of all.

Bread Machine		
A	P	Action
5		Preparation
15		Assemble & Weigh
5	85	Dough Prep
	----	1st Rise
25		Shaping
	0	Final Rise
10	5	Bake & Broil
5	0	Cool
65	90	TOTAL
1:05	1:30	2 hrs 35 min

%	Ingredient	Volume	Grams	Volume	Grams
			300.0		**600.0**
42.53	Water	1/3C+3Tbs+2tsp	127.58	1C+2Tb	255.18
18.9	Plain yogurt	1/4C	56.7	1/2C	113.4
4.73	Unsalted butter; melted	1Tb	14.18	2Tb	28.36
4.78	Honey (pourable)	2tsp	14.33	1Tb+1tsp	28.66
2.0	Salt	1tsp	6.0	2tsp	12.0
100.0	All-Purpose flour	2 1/3C+1Tb	300.0	4 3/4C +1Tb	600.0
1.04	Rapid rise yeast	1tsp	3.11	2tsp	6.22
175.98	**TOTAL**		**527.9**		**1055.82**
	FOR THE TOPPING				
	Garlic clove; minced	1 Whole	6.0	2 Whole	12.0
	Unsalted butter or Ghee*; melted	2Tbs		4Tbs	

Hydration = (255.18g+113.4g)/600g = 368.58g/600g = .6143 or 61.43%

Ghee is a form of butter that is an integral part of traditional Indian cuisine. It is clarified butter, which means that the water and milk solids (mostly proteins) have been boiled off, leaving just the rich, golden butterfat.

Preparation
- Be sure to review the recipe, and your machine's requirements before proceeding.
- Assemble and weigh/measure all ingredients. It will make your work much easier to have all weighed/measured and ready to follow directions.
- <u>Liquid Mix</u>: Combine <u>water</u>, <u>plain yogurt</u>, <u>melted unsalted butter</u>, <u>honey (clear/runny)</u>, and <u>salt</u> in a medium (large if mixing by Hand) bowl, or use the bread pan fitted with the kneading paddle if utilizing the Bread Machine.

Bread Machine
- Add the <u>Liquid Mix</u> to the bread pan fitted with the kneading paddle. Cover with the <u>flour</u>, and make a small, shallow hole in the center and add in the <u>yeast</u>.

- Place the bread pan in the bread maker. Press *Menu* and select *Dough Cycle*. Select *1* lb (*300g* flour) or *2* lb (*600g* flour) loaf. Press *Start* to mix, knead, and rise. Total Time = *1:25* for *300g flour*; *1:40* for *600g flour*.

- When Dough Cycle is complete, turn dough out on to a lightly floured work surface, and gently punch it down. Turn the machine off.

Prep & Shape
- Preheat oven to maximum setting; at least *450°F/232.2°C*.

- Depending on flour weight, divide dough into *3* or *6* equal pieces, and shape each into a small ball. Take one ball to work with, and cover remaining dough balls with a clean towel. Shape the working ball into an oval, circle or teardrop (about *1/4* inch thick).

- Cover shaped dough with the clean towel, and repeat shaping for another ball, and again cover the shaped dough. Continue the process until all the balls are shaped.

Prep & Bake
- For The Topping: Place <u>unsalted butter</u> and <u>minced garlic</u> into a ramekin and microwave to melt the butter. Stir garlic and melted butter together. Or, use stovetop to gently melt the butter and garlic together.

36 Delicious Direct Breads

- Using your peel. place the Naan on the preheated baking (pizza) stone and bake for *4-5* minutes. We have two baking stones in our oven and can do up to four at a time, depending on size. If there are more Naan than available space, bake as many times as needed, being sure to wait a few minutes between each batch to allow the stone to return to proper temperature.

- Remove and brush the Naan with melted butter & garlic mixture or Ghee & garlic mix; serve warm.

Notes

Moroccan KESRA[22]

Bread Machine		
A	P	Action
5		Preparation
15		Assemble & Weigh
5	90	Dough Prep
	----	1st Rise
20		Shaping
	30	Final Rise
5	25	Bake
5	30	Cool
5	175	TOTAL
0:55	2:55	3 hrs 50 min

Traditional Moroccan flatbread that goes good with stews, salads, cheeses or dips. If you want an Moroccan original, find a recipe for "*tagine*," a wonderful spicy stew. Or more correctly, a Moroccan stew prepared in a specially shaped clay pot and cover called a *tagine*.

Inspired by numerous Internet recipes

%	Ingredient	Volume	Grams	Volume	Grams
			400.0		*800.0*
53.75	Water	3/4C+3Tb+1/2tsp	215.0	1 3/4C+2Tb+1tsp	430.0
0.5	Granulated sugar	1/2tsp	2.0	1tsp	4.0
2.25	Salt	1 1/2tsp	9.0	1Tbs	18.0
67.5	Unbleached white bread flour	2 1/4C	270.0	4 1/2C	540.0
32.5	Semolina flour	3/4C+2tsp	130.0	1 1/2C+2TSP	260.0
0.58	Anise seed	1tsp	2.33	2tsp	4.66
0.78	Rapid rise yeast	1tsp	3.11	2tsp	6.22
157.86	**TOTAL**		**631.44**		**1262.58**
	FOR THE TOPPING				
	Olive Oil	1Tbs	15.0	2Tbs	30.0
	Sesame seeds	For Sprinkling			

Hydration = *430g/(540g+260g) = 430g/800g = .5375 or 53.75%*

Preparation

- Be sure to review the recipe, and your machine's requirements before proceeding.
- Assemble and weigh/measure all ingredients. It will make your work much easier to have all weighed/measured and ready to follow directions.

---

[22] *Kesra* is the Tamazight (Moroccan Berber People) word for bread.

38 Delicious Direct Breads

- <u>Liquid Mix</u>: Mix <u>water</u>, <u>sugar</u>, and <u>salt</u> in medium (large if mixing by Hand) bowl, or use the bread pan fitted with the kneading paddle if utilizing the Bread Machine.
- <u>Flour Mix</u>: Combine the <u>bread flour</u>, <u>semolina</u>, and <u>aniseed</u> together in a bowl.

Bread Machine

- Pour the <u>Liquid Mix</u> into the bread pan fitted with the kneading paddle and then cover with the <u>Flour Mix</u>. Make a shallow hole in the center and put in the <u>yeast</u>.

- Place the bread pan in the bread maker. Press *Menu* and select *Dough Cycle*. Select *1* lb (*400g* flour) or *2* lb (*800g* flour). Press *Start* to mix, knead, and rise. Total Time = *1:25* for *1* lb loaf; *1:40* for *2* lb loaf. You will need to assist the mixing and kneading, especially when preparing the *800g* of flour formula. It will initially be a gnarly and sticky mass but with assistance it will tighten up in about *15* minutes. It will eventually be supple and smooth.

- **For *400g* total flour**: When Cycle is complete, gently punch down dough and turn out on a floured work surface. Turn the bread machine off. ***Go To Prep & Shape.***

- **For *800g* total flour**: When mixing/kneading is done (*1:05* on timer), remove the dough from the bread pan and turn out on a floured surface. Turn the bread machine off. Remove the kneading paddle (if stuck into the dough) and shape the dough into a ball. Place in the oiled bowl (large enough to handle the doubling of the dough), and turn to coat all of the dough. Cover with plastic wrap and place in a warm place to rise for *45-60* minutes, or until just about double in bulk.

- When ready, gently punch down dough and turn out on a floured work surface.

Prep & Shape

- Divide the dough into two or four equal pieces depending on recipe size, and gently shape each into a ball. Flatten each to *3/4* inch thick discs. Place on lightly floured or parchment lined baking sheets.

- Cover with lightly oiled plastic wrap, and place in a warm place to rise for *45* minutes, or until doubled in bulk. Meanwhile preheat oven to *400°F/204.4°C*.

Prep & Bake

- When risen, brush the tops of each piece of dough with <u>olive oil</u>, and sprinkle with <u>sesame seeds</u>. With a skewer, prick the surface of the dough a number of times.

- Bake for *20-25* minutes, or until golden and sound hollow when tapped on the bottom. Turn out on a wire rack to cool.

Notes

Herb Focaccia

Unlike pizza dough, the rise time for focaccia is much longer creating a thicker bread. Also, unlike pizza, it is most often topped with a full layer of herbs, spices or meat.

Adapted From Cuisinart[23]

Bread Machine		
A	P	Action
5		Preparation
15		Assemble & Weigh
5	90	Dough Prep
	----	1st Rise
15	10	Shaping
10	40	2nd Rise
5	20	Bake
5	5	Cool
60	165	TOTAL
1:00	2:45	3 hrs 45 min

%	Ingredient	Volume	Grams	Volume	Grams
			270.0		**540.0**
63.0	Water	3/4C	170.0	1 1/2C	340.0
8.33	Extra virgin olive oil	1 1/2 Tbs	22.5	3 Tbs	45.0
2.23	Granulated sugar	1/2Tbs	6.0	1Tbs	12.0
2.22	Sea Salt	1 tsp	6.0	2 tsp	12.0
100.0	Unbleached white bread flour	2 1/8C	270.0	4 1/2C	540.0
0.56	Italian herb blend	1 1/2 tsp	1.5	1 Tbs	3.0
1.15	Rapid rise yeast	1tsp	3.11	2 tsp	6.22
176.89	**TOTAL**		**479.11**		**958.22**
	FOR THE TOPPING				
	Extra virgin olive oil	2 Tbs	30.0	1/4C	60.0
	Coarse Kosher or Sea Salt	1/2 tsp	6.0	1 tsp	6.0
	Freshly grated Asiago or Parmesan cheese	1/4C	56.7	1/3C	113.4
	Chopped fresh herbs (parsley, basil, oregano, thyme, marjoram) - loosely packed	3 Tbs		1/3C	

Hydration = 340g/540g = .6296 or 62.96%

---

[23] CBK-200 Cuisinart Convection Bread Maker; *Recipe Booklet*, 55.

Preparation
- Be sure to review the recipe, and your machine's requirements before proceeding.
- Assemble and weigh/measure all ingredients. It will make your work much easier to have all weighed/measured and ready to follow directions.
- Ensure water at *80°F/26.7°C – 90°F/32.2°C*.
- Liquid Mix: Mix the water, olive oil, sugar and salt in a medium (large if mixing by Hand) bowl, or use the bread pan fitted with the kneading paddle if utilizing the Bread Machine.
- Flour Mix: Combine the bread flour and Italian herb blend seasoning in a bowl.
- Our Italian herb blend: One teaspoon each of dried: oregano; basil; parsley; thyme and 1 tsp of granulated garlic. *About 1 gram per teaspoon.*

Bread Machine
- Place the Liquid Mix in the bread pan fitted with kneading paddle and then cover with the Flour Mix. Make a shallow hole in the center and put in the yeast.

- Place the bread pan in the bread maker. Press *Menu* and select *Dough Cycle*. Select *1* lb (*270g* flour) or *2* lb (*540g* flour). Press *Start* to mix, knead, and rise. Total Time = *1:25* for *1* lb loaf; *1:40* for *2* lb loaf.

- When the cycle has finished, remove the dough from the pan and place it on a lightly floured surface. Gently punch down. **Go To Continue All.**

Prep & Shape
- Divide dough into *2* or *4* equal pieces depending on recipe size. Cover with a towel and let rest for *10* minutes.

- After dough has rested, roll (or press out) out on a lightly floured surface to the desired shape. Place on parchment lined baking sheet and cover loosely with plastic wrap and let rise in a warm place until about doubled in size, about *45-60* minutes. Meanwhile, preheat oven to *450°F/232.2°C*.

Prep & Bake
- Uncover the risen focaccia, and, using your oiled fingertips, poke the dough to make deep dimples over the surface of the dough, about one inch apart. Drizzle with olive oil and sprinkle evenly with salt, cheese and herbs.

42 Delicious Direct Breads

- Bake until deep golden and puffed up with a crispy crust (about *10-20* minutes, depending on size).

- Remove and place on wire rack to cool slightly. Serve warm.

Notes

Pizza

Bread Machine		
A	P	Action
5		Preparation
15		Assemble & Weigh
5	100	Dough Prep
	----	1st Rise
20		Shaping
	0	Final Rise
15	20	Bake
5	0	Cool
65	125	TOTAL
1:05	2:00	3 hrs 5 min

Our favorite is a New York style thin crust pizza. Just the right amount of cheese, and a bit more oil than is often found on others. Never eaten with a fork, you simply fold it lengthwise and flip up the tip to keep the oil from spilling onto the plate.

%	Ingredient	Volume	Grams	Volume	Grams
		Small	*250.0*	Regular	*500.0*
58.59	Water	1/2C+2Tb+1tsp	146.48	1 1/4 C +2tsp	292.95
6.0	Extra virgin olive oil	1 Tbs	15.0	2 Tbs	30.0
0.8	Granulated sugar	1/2 tsp	2.0	1 tsp	4.0
2.4	Salt	1 tsp	6.0	2 tsp	12.0
100	Unbleached white bread flour	2 1/8 C	250.0	4 1/8 C	500.0
0.93	Rapid rise yeast	3/4 tsp	2.33	1 1/2 tsp	4.67
168.72	TOTAL		415.81		832.12

Hydration = *292.95g/500g = .5859 or 58.59%*

Preparation

- Be sure to review the recipe, and your machine's requirements before proceeding.
- Assemble and weigh/measure all ingredients. It will make your work much easier to have all weighed/measured and ready to follow directions.
- Ensure water at *80°F/26.7°C – 90°F/32.2°C.*
- <u>Liquid Mix</u>: Mix <u>water</u>, <u>olive oil</u>, <u>sugar</u> and <u>salt</u> in medium bowl (large if mixing by Hand) bowl, or use the bread pan fitted with the kneading paddle if utilizing the Bread Machine.

44 Delicious Direct Breads

Bread Machine
- Place the <u>Liquid Mix</u> in the bread pan fitted with kneading paddle and then cover with the <u>flour</u>. Make a shallow hole in the center and put in the <u>yeast</u>.

- Place the bread pan in the bread maker. Press *Menu* and select *Dough Cycle*. Select *1* lb (*250g* flour) or *2* lb (*500g* flour). Press *Start* to mix, knead, and rise. Total Time = *1:25* for *1* lb loaf; *1:40* for *2* lb loaf.

- *Note*: If you are using the "small" weights, be sure to check the mixing/kneading of the dough during the first five minutes. You may need to assist in the mixing by scraping the sides, etc.

- When dough cycle is complete, remove dough and place onto a floured surface; gently punch down.

Prep & Shape
- Preheat oven to *425°F/218.3°C*.

- Divide in two if using *500g* recipe. Shape into a round about *1/8* inch thick, or more if you want a thicker crust. Place on pizza pan, or on peel to place directly on the pizza/baking stone.

- Lightly coat dough with <u>olive oil</u> and cover with your chosen sauce. Continue by adding desired toppings.

Bake
- Bake *15-20* minutes or until golden and sizzling. Serve immediately.

Alternate Baking
- Preheat oven to maximum. We use *500°F/260°C*. Bake *10-12* minutes or till the edge is golden brown and the cheese is bubbly and golden. Lift bottom with spatula to check crust being golden brown. If the crust needs more time, but the cheese is browning, cover with aluminum foil or parchment paper to give it more time.

- Remove from oven and serve immediately.

Notes

French

Baguette Basic & Pure

To be sold as a baguette in France, the law states that a baguette can only contain water, flour, salt and yeast. Add anything else, and it can't be marketed or sold as a baguette.

Bread Machine		
A	P	Action
5		Preparation
15		Assemble & Weigh
5	100	Dough Prep
	----	1st Rise
20	10	Shaping
	60	Final Rise
5	25	Bake
5	30	Cool
55	225	TOTAL
0:55	3:45	4 hrs 40 min

%	Ingredient	Volume	Grams	Volume	Grams
			400.0		**800.0**
65.0	Water; lukewarm	1C+2Tb+1tsp	260.0	2 1/4C+2tsp	520.0
1.69	Salt	1 1/8 tsp	6.75	2 1/4 tsp	13.5
80.5	Unbleached white bread flour	2 2/3C+1 1/2tsp	322.0	5 1/3 C	644.0
19.5	All-purpose flour	2/3 C	78.0	1 1/4 C	156.0
0.88	Rapid rise yeast	1 1/8 tsp	3.5	2 1/4 tsp	7.0
167.57	TOTAL		670.25		1340.5

Hydration = 520g/(644g+156g) = 520g/800g = .65 or 65.0%

Preparation

- Be sure to review the recipe, and your machine's requirements/limitations before proceeding.
- Assemble and weigh/measure all ingredients. It will make your work much easier to have all weighed/measured and ready to follow directions.
- <u>Liquid Mix</u>: Mix <u>water</u> and <u>salt</u> in a medium (large if mixing by Hand) bowl, or use the bread pan fitted with the kneading paddle if utilizing the Bread Machine.
- <u>Flour Mix</u>: In a separate bowl, mix <u>bread</u> and <u>all-purpose flours</u>.
- *Be aware! This hydration results in a sticky/gnarly dough.*

Bread Machine

- Place the <u>Liquid Mix</u> in the bread pan fitted with kneading paddle and then cover with the <u>Flour Mix</u>. Make a shallow hole in the center and put in the <u>yeast</u>.

48 Delicious Direct Breads

- Place the bread pan in the bread maker. Press *Menu* and select *Dough Cycle*. Select *1* lb (*400g* flour) or *2* lb (*800g* flour). Press *Start* to mix, knead, and rise. Total Time = *1:25* for *1* lb loaf; *1:40* for *2* lb loaf. You will need to assist the mixing and kneading, especially if you are preparing the *800g* of flour formula.

- **For *400g* total flour**: When Cycle is complete, gently punch down dough and turn out on a floured work surface. Turn the bread machine off. ***Go To Prep & Shape.***

- **For *800g* total flour**: When mixing/kneading is done (*1:05* on timer), remove the dough from the bread pan and turn out on a floured surface. Turn the bread machine off. Remove the kneading paddle (if stuck into the dough) and shape the dough into a ball. Place in the oiled bowl (large enough to handle the doubling of the dough), and turn to coat all of the dough. Cover with plastic wrap and place in a warm place to rise for *45- 60* minutes, or until just about double in bulk.

- When ready, gently punch down dough and turn out on a floured work surface.

Prep & Shape

- Divide dough into desired size loaves. Some like smaller and "thinner" like *200* grams per loaf, while others like a "thicker" baguette using *300* grams. Experiment and decide for yourself.

- Fold the bottom third up lengthways and the top third down and press down to make sure the pieces of dough are in contact. Seal the edges. Repeat two or three more times until each loaf is an oblong. Leave to rest *10* minutes in between folding to avoid tearing the dough.

- Gently stretch each piece of dough lengthways into a *13 to 14* inch long loaf. Pleat a floured dish towel on a baking sheet to make two moulds for the loaves (Or use banneton). Place the breads between the pleats of the towel, to help hold their shape while rising. Cover with lightly oiled plastic wrap and leave to rise, in a warm place, for *45* to *60* minutes. Meanwhile, prepare oven for *Hearth Baking*, and preheat to maximum, at least *450°F/232.2°C*. We use *500°F/260°C*.

Prep & Bake

- Roll the loaves onto a baking sheet, spaced well apart. Using a sharp knife, slash the top of each loaf several times with long diagonal slits.

- Place baking sheet in the oven and add *1* cup of ice cubes to the preheated cast iron pan. Bake for *20* to *25* minutes, or until golden (time will be a bit longer if less than *500°F/260°C*). *After 10 minutes of baking, remove the pan containing the water from the ice cubes. From this point on we want dry heat.*

- When golden brown, remove and check internal temperature; *195°F/90.6°C – 210°F/98.9°C* at sea level. - Transfer to a wire rack to cool. Best taste and flavor after *30 - 60* minutes of cooling.

Notes

Brioche

Bread Machine		
A	P	Action
5		Preparation
15		Assemble & Weigh
5	100	Dough Prep
	----	1st Rise
10	60	Refrigerate
20		Shape
	45	Final Rise
5	30	Bake
5	30	Cool
65	265	TOTAL
1:05	4:25	5 hrs 30 min

A enriched French creation with high egg and butter content that results in a rich and tender crumb. The egg wash contributes to its golden crust.

Adapted From Cuisinart[24]

%	Ingredient	Volume	Grams	Volume	Grams
			225.0		**450.0**
25.2	Milk 80°F-90°F	1/4 C	56.7	1/2C	113.4
41.78	Large Eggs	2	94.0	4	188.0
25.2	Butter	4 Tbs	56.7	8 Tbs	113.4
5.33	Sugar	1 Tbs	12.0	2 Tbs	24.0
2.0	Salt	3/4 tsp	4.5	1 1/2 tsp	9.0
100.0	Unbleached bread flour	1 3/4C+2Tbs	225.0	3 3/4 C	450.0
2.67	Powdered milk	1 Tbs	6.0	2 Tbs	12.0
2.07	Rapid rise yeast	1 1/2 tsp	4.67	3 tsp	9.33
204.25	**TOTAL**		**459.57**		**919.13**
	Egg Wash	1 large egg beaten with 1 Tbs water		1 large egg beaten with 1 Tbs water	

Hydration = *(113.4g+188g)/450g = 301.4g/450g = .6698 or 66.98%*

Preparation

- Assemble and weigh/measure all ingredients. It will make your work much easier to have all weighed/measured and ready to follow directions.

---

[24] CBK-200 Cuisinart Convection Bread Maker; *Recipe Booklet*, 50.

- All ingredients at room temperature unless otherwise specified.
- Ensure milk at *80°F/26.7°C – 90°F/32.2°C.*
- Liquid Mix: Mix milk, eggs, melted butter, sugar and salt in medium (large if mixing by Hand) bowl, or use the bread pan fitted with the kneading paddle if utilizing the Bread Machine.
- Flour Mix: Mix powdered milk and the flour together in a large mixing bowl.

Bread Machine

- Place the Liquid Mix in the bread pan fitted with kneading paddle and then cover with the Flour Mix. Make a shallow hole in the center and put in the yeast.

- Place the bread pan in the bread maker. Press *Menu* and select *Dough Cycle*. Select *1* lb (*225g* flour) or *2* lb (*450g* flour). Press *Start* to mix, knead, and rise. Total Time = *1:25* for *1* lb loaf; *1:40* for *2* lb loaf.

- Keep an eye on the dough development ten minutes into the kneading. If necessary, pause the machine and scrape the sides of the pan to ensure even distribution of ingredients. When dough cycle is complete, remove dough and place onto a floured surface.

Prep & Shape

- Deflate dough, and put into a well-buttered bowl. Cover with plastic wrap and refrigerate for one hour, or overnight. When ready, shape right out of the refrigerator.

- Deflate dough and divide into the number and size brioches desired. For *1* lb brioche, remove *1/6* of the dough and shape the remainder into a ball and press into a buttered *6*-inch brioche mold. Press a hole in the center about *1* inch deep. Shape the smaller piece into a ball and place in the center hole.

- Cover loosely with plastic wrap and rise in a warm (*90°F/32.2°C*) draft-free place for about *45* minutes. Meanwhile, preheat oven to *350°F/176.7°C*. Be sure to use lowest or next to lowest rack level to allow for significant rise.

Bake

- Brush brioche(s) with egg wash. Bake for *20* to *30* minutes, until rich golden in color and hollow-sounding when tapped. Remove from pans and transfer to wire rack to cool.

Notes

Pain Ordinaire

{ This is a French white bread that is simple to prepare. It is usually made with only yeast, bread flour or all-purpose flour, water, and salt. You will see that this is very similar to a French baguette recipe, but *pain ordinaire* contains a little less water and yeast. It is a "flexible" loaf in that you can find it being done in a variety of shapes. }

Bread Machine		
A	P	Action
5		Preparation
15		Assemble & Weigh
5	100	Dough Prep
	----	1st Rise
15	30	Shaping
5	720	Refrig Overnight
5	60	Room Temp
5	30	Bake
	30	Cool
55	970	TOTAL
0:55	16:10	17 hrs 05 min

%	Ingredient	Volume	Grams	Volume	Grams
			300.0		**600.0**
60.0	water	3/4C+1/2Tbs+1/2tsp	180.0	1 1/2C+1Tbs+1tsp	360.0
2.0	salt	1tsp	6.0	2tsp	12.0
50.0	Unbleached all-purpose flour	1C+3Tbs	150.0	2 1/3C	300.0
50.0	Unbleached bread flour	1 1/4C	150.0	2 1/2C	300.0
0.50	Rapid rise yeast	1/2tsp	1.5	1tsp	3.0
162.5	TOTAL		487.5		975.0

Hydration = *360g/(300g+300g) = 360g/600g = .60 or 60.0%*

Preparation

- Assemble and weigh/measure all ingredients. It will make your work much easier to have all weighed/measured and ready to follow directions.
- Ensure water at *65°F/18.3°C – 70°F/21.1°C*.
- Liquid Mix: Mix water and salt in medium (large if mixing by Hand) bowl, or use the bread pan fitted with the kneading paddle if utilizing the Bread Machine.
- Flour Mix: Blend the two flours together in a large mixing bowl.

Delicious Direct Breads

Bread Machine
- Place the Liquid Mix in the bread pan fitted with kneading paddle and then cover with the Flour Mix. Make a shallow hole in the center and put in the yeast.

- Place the bread pan in the bread maker. Press *Menu* and select *Dough Cycle*. Select *1* lb (*300g* flour) or *2* lb (*600g* flour). Press *Start* to mix, knead, and rise. Total Time = *1:25* for *1* lb loaf; *1:40* for *2* lb loaf.

- When dough cycle is complete, remove dough and place onto a floured surface. *Go To* **Continue All.**

Prep & Shape
- *Bench*, and *shape* the dough. I typically shape it into a boule (round loaf). Place shaped dough on lightly greased or parchment lined baking sheet, and cover with lightly oiled plastic wrap and let it rest for *30* minutes. Place the covered baking sheet in a large plastic bag and refrigerate overnight.

Next Day
- Remove the dough from the refrigerator but leave it in the bag. The dough should have risen approximately *50* percent, and if it has, let the dough sit out for *1* hour to take off the chill. If not fully risen, let it sit at room temperature for *2* or *3* hours, until it completes its rise.

- Prepare oven for *Hearth Baking* and preheat to *475°F/246.1°C* (allow about *45* minutes for it to heat fully.) Make sure your spritzer bottle is filled with water.

Prep & Bake
- Remove the pan of dough from the plastic bag *15* minutes before baking, to allow the surface of the dough to dry slightly. Just before baking, dock the bread. Place baking sheet with shaped dough on the pizza stone. Dump *1* cup of ice cubes in the preheated cast iron pan, and close the oven door promptly.

- After *2* minutes, quickly spray the oven walls and the bread again. Repeat in *2* minutes. Then lower the oven temperature to *450°F/232.2°C*.

- After *10* minutes, remove the cast iron pan filled with water, and check the bread. Rotate the bread, front to back, if it seems to be baking unevenly. (If baking on more than one oven rack, rotate the bread top to bottom as well.)

- When the bread has developed a rich, golden brown color -- this will take about *25* minutes, remove and check temperature. When done it will be about *200°F/93.3°C – 205°F/96.1°C*.

- When you are satisfied, turn off the oven (or lower to *350°F/176.7°C* if you plan to bake again) and leave the bread in the oven an additional *5* minutes, until it seems on the verge of overbrowning.

- Remove the bread to a cooling rack and allow it to cool thoroughly before eating; about *30* to *45* minutes.

Notes

German

Pumpernickel Raisin Walnut Bread

With or without walnuts, this is a wonderful bread. A favorite of our Bridge Club, it has become one of our most requested breads.

Adapted From: Cuisinart[25]

%	Ingredient	Volume	Grams	Volume	Grams
			400.0		**800.0**
60.0	Water	1C+1Tbs	240.0	2C+2Tbs	480.0
1.875	Salt	1 1/4 tsp	7.5	2 1/2 tsp	15.44
18.35	Molasses	3Tb+1 1/4tsp	73.4	1/3C+1Tbs+1 1/2tsp	146.8
3.5	Vegetable oil	1 Tbs	14.0	1Tbs+2 1/2tsp	28.0
67.5	Unbleached white bread flour	2 1/4 C	270.0	4 1/2 C	540.0
13.0	Whole-wheat flour	1/3C+1tbs+2tsp	52.0	3/4C+2Tbs	104.0
10.0	Rye flour	1/3C+1Tbs	40.0	3/4C1tsp+3/4tsp	80.0
9.5	Cornmeal	1/4C+2 1/4tsp	38.0	1/2C+1tsp	76.0
3.125	Vital wheat gluten	1Tbs+2Tsp	12.5	3Tbs+1Tsp	25.0
2.5	Unsweetened cocoa powder	2 Tbs	10.0	1/4 C	20.0
0.885	Instant espresso powder	2 tsp	3.54	1Tbs+1tsp	7.08
1.50	Rapid rise yeast	1 3/4 tsp	6.0	1Tbs+3/4tsp	12.0
21.32	raisins	1/2C+1Tbs+1/2tsp	85.28	1C+2Tbs+1tsp	170.56
1.333	Caraway seeds	2 tsp	5.33	1Tbs+1tsp	10.66
7.09	Walnuts; chopped	1/4 C	28.35	1/2 C	56.7
221.48	**TOTAL**		886.12		1772.24

Hydration = 480g/(540g+104g+80g+76g) = 480g/800g = .6 or 60.0%

---

[25] CBK-200 Cuisinart Convection Bread Maker; *Recipe Booklet*, 19.

Bread Machine		
A	P	Action
5		Preparation
15		Assemble & Weigh
10	35	Dough Prep
	45	1st Rise
15	15	Shaping
	60	Final Rise
5	40	Bake
5	30	Cool
55	225	TOTAL
0:55	3:45	4 hrs 40 min

Note: You do not include molasses in the hydration as it doesn't contain any water. It is *100%* sugar. But you need to add the cornmeal to the flour total.

Preparation

- Be sure to review the formula, and your machine's requirements before proceeding. Assemble and weigh/measure all ingredients. It will make your work much easier to have all weighed/measured and ready to follow directions.
- Ensure water at *85°F/29.4°C – 95°F/35°C*.
- Liquid Mix: Mix water, salt, molasses and vegetable oil in a medium (large if mixing by Hand) bowl, or use the bread pan fitted with the kneading paddle if utilizing the Bread Machine.
- Flour Mix: - Combine flours with vital wheat gluten, cornmeal, cocoa powder, and espresso powder.

Bread Machine

- Coat bread machine kneading paddle with vegetable oil to help prevent sticking.

- Place the Liquid Mix in the bread pan fitted with kneading paddle and then cover with the Flour Mix. Make a shallow hole in the center and put in the yeast.

- Place the bread pan in the bread maker. Press *Menu* and select *Dough Cycle*. Select *1* lb (*400g* flour) or *2* lb (*800g* flour). Press *Start* to mix, knead, and rise. Total Time = *1:25* for *1* lb loaf; *1:40* for *2* lb loaf. You will need to assist the mixing and kneading, especially if you are preparing the *800g* of flour formula.

- When Mix-in's tone sounds *(1 lb loaf = 1:12; 2 lb loaf = 1:19 Remaining),* add raisins, chopped walnuts and caraway seeds. I have found that I need to monitor the "gathering" of the raisins and walnuts. I use a spatula to aid the dough in taking up the ingredients. I have even paused the machine. to spread the dough a bit and turned it back on. Just be sure that all added ingredients have been mixed well.

- **For *400g* total flour**: When Cycle is complete, gently punch down dough and turn out on a floured work surface. Turn the bread machine off. ***Go To Prep & Shape.***

- **For *800g* total flour**: When mixing/kneading is done (*1:05* on timer), remove the dough from the bread pan and turn out on a floured surface. Turn the bread machine off. Remove the kneading paddle (if stuck into the dough) and shape the dough into a ball. Place in the oiled bowl (large enough to handle the doubling of the dough), and turn to coat all of the dough. Cover with plastic wrap and place in a warm place to rise for *45-60* minutes, or until just about double in bulk.

- When ready, gently punch down dough and turn out on a floured work surface.

Prep & Shape

- Lightly oil one or two *2* lb loaf pans/tins (*7 1/4" x 4 1/2"*).

- Check ingredients are uniformly mixed throughout the dough by gently kneading several times, or more if necessary. If doing large dough, divide in half and prepare two loaves.

- I shape this dough different from the usual letter-fold. Shape by hand by patting the dough into a thick rectangle, roughly the size of the bottom of the pan. It helps to hold the dough up by the short end to use the weight of the dough to lengthen itself. If necessary, let the dough rest for *10* minutes before continuing.

- When the dough is approximately the size of the bottom of the pan, place it in the oiled pan and using your fingers, and knuckles, press it to the shape of the pan.

- Cover with plastic wrap and let rise for *45* minutes, or until double in bulk. Meanwhile, preheat oven to *400°F/204.4°C*. There is little to no oven-spring so the height you see now, will be the final size loaf.

Bake

- When dough is ready, bake for about *40 minutes*. **After *5* minutes, reduce oven temperature to *375°F/190.6°C*.**

- I use an instant read thermometer, looking for *195°F/90.56°C – 205°F/96.11°C*, and I check the probe for any dough, just like using a cake tester. Remove from oven and transfer to a wire rack to cool. Sufficiently cooling the Bread allows the flavors to develop and it makes it easier to slice.

Notes

Rye Bread: Lynne's Grandmother

This recipe has undergone several trials, and the result is a wonderful bread with slightly crisp crust, a tasty light crumb with just the right amount of "chewy." At the Suggestion of Lynne's Father (Grandma's Son) we increased the amount of Caraway seeds. He said: *"When I was a kid, you could put your thumb anywhere on the slice of bread and there would be a caraway seed. This is close, but a bit more should do it."* Contrast with "Rye With Caraway" in "Our Daily Breads."

Bread Machine		
A	P	Action
5		Preparation
15		Assemble & Weigh
10	35	Dough Prep
	60	1st Rise
20		Shaping
	45	Final Rise
5	40	Bake
5	30	Cool
60	210	TOTAL
1:00	3:30	4 hrs 30 min

Adapted from Lynn's Grandmother's Rye Bread.

%	Ingredient	Volume	Grams	Volume	Grams
			400.0		**800.0**
63.0	Milk; 85-95F	1C+1Tb	252.0	2C+2Tb	504.0
2.5	Salt	1 3/4 tsp	10.0	1Tb+1/3tsp	20.0
9.0	Grandma's Gold Label Molasses	1Tb+2tsp	36.0	3Tb+1tsp	72.0
1.7	Sugar	1/2 Tb	6.8	1 Tb	13.6
1.7	Vegetable shortening; melted	1/2 Tb	6.8	1 Tb	13.6
78.0	Unbleached white bread flour	1C+ 1 3/4Tb	312.0	5 1/4C	624.0
22.0	Rye flour	3/4C+1Tb+1tsp	88.0	1 3/4C	176.0
1.5	Rapid rise yeast	2tsp	6.0	3 3/4tsp	12.0
3.0	Caraway seeds	1 1/2 Tb	12.0	3 Tb	24.0
182.4	TOTAL		729.6		1459.2

Hydration = 504g/(624g+176g) = 504g/800g = .63 or 63.0%

The recipe has been reduced in amount or "size" so as to be appropriate for today's bread machines and food processors. **Many thanks go to Lynne's family, especially to her grandmother.**

62 Delicious Direct Breads

Preparation
- Be sure to review the recipe, and your machine's requirements before proceeding.
- Assemble and weigh/measure all ingredients. It will make your work much easier to have all weighed/measured and ready to follow directions.
- Remember to cover anything melted/softened in the microwave with a paper towel.
- Place Milk in microwave on high for *40* seconds. Want it to be *85°F/29.4°C – 95°F/35°C*.
- Place shortening in microwave on high for about *30* seconds or until fully melted.
- Liquid Mix: Mix warm milk, salt, molasses, sugar, and melted shortening in a medium (large if mixing by Hand) bowl, or use the bread pan fitted with the kneading paddle if utilizing the Bread Machine.
- Flour Mix: In a large bowl, combine white and rye flours.

Bread Machine
- Pour the Liquid Mix in the bread pan fitted with kneading paddle and then cover with the Flour Mix. Make a shallow hole in the center and put in the yeast.

- Place the bread pan in the bread maker. Press *Menu* and select *Dough Cycle*. Select *1* lb (*400g* flour) or *2* lb (*800g* flour). Press *Start* to mix, knead, and rise. Total Time = *1:25* for *1* lb loaf; *1:40* for *2* lb loaf. You will need to assist the mixing and kneading, especially if you are preparing the *800g* of flour formula. It will initially be a gnarly and sticky mass but with assistance it will tighten up in about *15* minutes. It will eventually be supple and smooth.

- When Mix-in's tone sounds (*1 lb loaf = 1:12; 2 lb loaf = 1:19 Remaining*), add caraway seeds .

- **For *400g* total flour**: When Cycle is complete, gently punch down dough and turn out on a floured work surface. Turn the bread machine off. ***Go To Prep & Shape.***

- **For *800g* total flour**: When mixing/kneading is done (*1:05* on timer), remove the dough from the bread pan and turn out on a floured surface. Turn the bread machine off. Remove the kneading paddle (if stuck into the dough) and shape the dough into a ball. Place in the oiled bowl (large enough to handle the doubling of the dough), and turn to coat all of the dough. Cover with plastic wrap and place in a warm place to rise for *45- 60* minutes, or until just about double in bulk.

- When ready, gently punch down dough and turn out on a floured work surface.

Prep & Shape

- Shape dough (If doing *800g* formula, divide dough into two equal pieces) into preferred shape. I like the "fat" torpedo shape which gives us nice small sandwich size slices.

- Place on a baking sheet lined with parchment paper; cover and let rise in a warm place until doubles in bulk (about *45* minutes). While waiting for last rise, prepare oven for *Hearth Baking*, and preheat to *450°F/232.2°C*.

Prep & Bake

- When dough is ready, Lightly make a *1/4"* cut lengthwise down the loaf. This will allow the loaf to expand. Place in preheated oven; add *1* cup of ice cubes to the cast iron pan; close the door and reduce the temperature to *425°F/218.3°C*.

Bake for *10* minutes, adding steam by spraying water into the oven 3 or 4 times. Then remove cast iron pan filled with water, and reduce temperature to *375°F/190.6°C* and bake for another *20-25* minutes. Bread should reach *200°F/93.3°C – 210°F/98.9°C* at sea level. For a rustic and chewy crust, place bread back in the "turned off" oven for *5* minutes.

- Remove and place on wire rack to cool. Best taste and flavor after *30 - 60* min of cooling.

Notes

Holiday

Cranberry Orange Nut Bread

Some like walnuts and others like pecans, but just about everyone loves the flavors of cranberry orange.

Adapted from: allrecipes.com; Paular[26]

%	Ingredient	Volume	Grams	Volume	Grams
			375.0		**750.0**
72.0	Orange juice	1 1/8C	270.0	2 1/4C	540.0
4.27	Vegetable oil	1Tbs	16.0	2Tbs	32.0
11.47	Honey	2Tbs	43.0	1/4C	86.0
1.6	Salt	1tsp	6.0	2tsp	12.0
100	Unbleached white bread flour	3C+2Tbs	375.0	6 1/4C	750.0
1.6	Non-fat dry milk	1Tbs	6.0	2Tbs	12.0
0.35	Ground cinnamon	1/2tsp	1.3	1tsp	2.6
0.27	Ground all-spice	1/2tsp	1.0	1tsp	2.0
2.13	Grated or dried orange zest	1Tbs	7.0	2Tbs	14.0
1.87	Active dry yeast	2 1/4tsp	7.0	4 1/2tsp	14.0
30.24	Sweetened dried cranberries	1C	113.4	2C	226.8
10.0	Chopped walnuts or Pecans	1/3C	37.8	2/3C	75.6
235.8	**TOTAL**		**883.5**		**1767.0**
	Sanding Sugar	Dusting		Dusting	
	OR Use Glaze				
	Fresh orange juice			2Tbs	28.35
	Caster sugar			2Tbs	28.13

Hydration = *540g/750g = .72 or 72.0%*

---

[26] " Paular "Cranberry Orange Breakfast Bread," *allrecipes.com*, Last Accessed 11/10/2017, http://allrecipes.com/Recipe/ Cranberry-Orange-Breakfast- Bread/Detail.aspx?event8=1&prop24=SR_Title&e11=cranberry%20orange%20walnut%20bread&e8=Quick%20Search&event10=1&e7=Recipe&soid=sr_results_p1i2

Preparation

Be sure to review the recipe, and your machine's requirements before proceeding.
- Assemble and weigh/measure all ingredients. It will make your work much easier to have all weighed/measured and ready to follow directions.
- Warm the orange juice in the microwave *(85°F/29.4°C – 95°F/35°C)*.
- Liquid Mix: Mix orange juice, vegetable oil, honey, and salt in medium (large if mixing by Hand) bowl, or use the bread pan fitted with the kneading paddle if utilizing the Bread Machine.

Bread Machine		
A	P	Action
5		Preparation
15		Assemble & Weigh
10	35	Dough Prep
	60	1st Rise
15	15	Shaping
	60	Final Rise
5	50	Bake
5	30	Cool
55	245	TOTAL
0:55	4:05	5 hrs 0 min

- Flour Mix: In a medium bowl, add the flour, nonfat dry milk, grated orange zest, ground cinnamon and ground allspice. Mix together.

Bread Machine

- Place the Liquid Mix, in the bread pan fitted with kneading paddle and then cover with the Flour Mix. Make a shallow hole in the center and put in the yeast.

- Place the bread pan in the bread maker. Press *Menu* and select *Dough Cycle*. Select *1* lb (*375g* flour) or *2* lb (*750g* flour). Press *Start* to mix, knead, and rise. Total Time = *1:25* for *1* lb loaf; *1:40* for *2* lb loaf. You will need to assist the mixing and kneading, especially if you are preparing the *800g* of flour formula. It will initially be a gnarly and sticky mass but with assistance it will tighten up in about *15* minutes. It will eventually be supple and smooth.

- When Mix-in's tone sounds (*1 lb loaf = 1:12; 2 lb loaf = 1:19 Remaining*), add cranberries and chopped walnuts, or pecans.

- **For *375g* total flour**: When Cycle is complete, gently punch down dough and turn out on a floured work surface. Turn the bread machine off. ***Go To Prep & Shape.***

- **For *750g* total flour**: When mixing/kneading is done (*1:05* on timer), remove the dough from the bread pan and turn out on a floured surface. Turn the bread machine off. Remove the kneading paddle (if stuck into the dough) and shape the dough into a ball. Place in the oiled bowl (large enough to handle the doubling of

Holiday 69

the dough), and turn to coat all of the dough. Cover with plastic wrap and place in a warm place to rise for *45- 60* minutes, or until just about double in bulk.

- When ready, gently punch down dough and turn out on a floured work surface.

Prep & Shape

- Lightly oil one or two *2* lb loaf pans/tins (*7 1/4" x 4 1/2"*), and preheat oven to *375°F/190.6°C.*

- Shape into an oblong about the width of the bread pan, and then use "letter fold" method. Roll the dough out so that it is the length of the bread pan, and *3* times its width. We found that it was best to let the dough rest for *15* minutes during this shaping. After rolling out, from the longer side, fold one third down, and then fold one third up. Tuck the ends in a bit and pinch all seams together to seal. Flip the loaf over, and with the seam on the bottom, place in the oiled bread pan and, if necessary, push slightly to have it fill the pan.

- Cover with plastic wrap and place in a warm place to rise until double in bulk; about *60* minutes.

Prep & Bake

- When ready, spray top of loaf with water and sprinkle with <u>Sanding Sugar</u> OR use <u>glaze</u> when on the rack to cool. Bake for *40 - 60* minutes. I cover with foil after *30-35* minutes to prevent browning from becoming too dark. Your particular desired appearance will dictate when to cover with the foil.

- Bread is ready when internal temperature reaches *190°F/87.8°C – 200°F/93.3°C.*

- Remove from pan and place on wire rack to cool. Sufficiently cooling the Bread allows the flavors to develop and it makes it easier to slice. If using the <u>glaze</u> place on top of loaf while it is still warm.

Notes

Hot Cross Buns

Made with currants or raisins, these are a spiced and sweet bun often prepared to celebrate Christian Easter, hence the cross on top.

In the event you do not have "apple pie spice" in your pantry, we have provided a recipe that works well.

Bread Machine		
A	P	Action
5		Preparation
15		Assemble & Weigh
10	100	Dough Prep
	----	1st Rise
20		Shaping
	45	Final Rise
5	22	Bake
10	30	Cool
65	197	TOTAL
1:05	3:17	4 hrs 22 min

Adapted From Food Network.com[27]

%	Ingredient	Volume	Grams	Volume	Grams
		6 Buns	**187.5**	**12 Buns**	**375.0**
30.24	water	1/4C	56.7	1/2C	113.4
32.0	Milk	1/4C	60.0	1/2C	120.0
25.6	sugar	1/4C	48.0	1/2C	96.0
20.16	Unsalted butter	2Tb+2tsp	37.8	1/3C	75.6
5.04	Egg Yoke	1/2 large	9.45	1 large	18.9
1.73	Vanilla extract	3/4tsp	3.25	1 1/2tsp	6.5
1.2	Sea Salt	1/3tsp	2.25	3/4tsp	4.5
100.0	Unbleached white All Purpose flour	1 1/2C	187.5	3C	375.0
0.85	Apple pie spice	2/3tsp	1.6	1 1/4tsp	3.2
3.73	Rapid rise yeast	1 2/3tsp	5.25	3 1/3tsp	10.5
12.6	Currants	3 Tb	23.63	1/3C	47.25
12.6	Raisins	3 Tb	23.63	1/3C	47.25
245.75	**TOTAL %**		**460.8**		**921.60**
	For The Glaze				
	Beaten Egg	1/2 large	23.5	1 large	47.0
	FOR THE PASTRY CROSSES				
	Confectioner Sugar	3/4C	78.0	1 1/2C	156.0
	Whole Milk	3/4 Tb	11.25	1 1/2Tb	22.5
	Pure Vanilla Extract	1/3tsp	1.63	3/4tsp	3.25

Hydration = (113.4g+120g+18.9g)/375g = 252.3g/375g = .6728 or 67.28%

---

[27] "Hot Cross Buns," *foodnetwork.com*, Last Accessed 11/10/2017, http://www.foodnetwork.com/recipes/food-network-kitchen/hot-cross-buns-recipe-1928112#!

Preparation

Apple Pie Spice: This mixture of sweet spices is perfect for adding an apple flavor to your baking and cooking.
- *1 tablespoon ground cinnamon 1-1/2 teaspoon ground nutmeg 1 teaspoon ground allspice 1/4 teaspoon ground cloves*. Store, tightly covered, in a cool dry place.
- Beat egg yoke.
- Melt butter in microwave.
- Liquid Mix: Combine water, milk, sugar, melted butter, beaten egg yolk, vanilla extract and salt in a large bowl, or use the bread pan fitted with the kneading paddle if utilizing the Bread Machine.
- Flour Mix: Combine flour and apple pie spice together.

Bread Machine

- Put the Liquid Mix in the bread pan fitted with the kneading paddle.

- Add the Flour Mix, ensuring that it covers the liquid. Make a shallow indent in the center and add the yeast.

- Place the bread pan in the bread maker. Press *Menu* and select *Dough Cycle*. Select *1* lb (*187.5g* flour) or *2* lb (*375g* flour). Press *Start* to mix, knead, and rise. Total Time = *1:25* for *1* lb loaf; *1:40* for *2* lb loaf.

- When the mix-in signal sounds *(1 lb loaf = 1:12; 2 lb loaf = 1:19 Remaining)*, add the currants, and raisins.

- When the dough cycle is complete, remove and place dough on a lightly floured surface.

Prep & Shape

- Lightly grease two baking sheets, or use parchment paper.

- Punch it down gently, and then divide it into *6* or *12* pieces. Cup each piece between your hands and shape it into a ball. Place on the prepared baking sheets, cover with oiled plastic wrap. Leave to rise for *45* minutes or until almost doubled in size.

- Meanwhile, preheat oven to *375°F/190.6°C*.

Prep & Bake

- When ready, remove plastic wrap and brush the beaten egg on the buns and bake for *20 to 22* minutes, or until golden and internal temperature is *195°F/90.6°C – 200°F/93.3°C*.

- Remove and place on a wire rack to cool.

- *Make the pastry for the crosses*. In a bowl, mix the milk, lemon zest, and vanilla extract together. Add this mixture to the confectioner sugar and mix well with a fork until a uniform and smooth icing is formed.

- When the buns are cool or barely warm, pipe the icing in the form of a cross on the buns.

Notes

Panettone Loaf

Bread Machine		
A	P	Action
5		Preparation
15		Assemble & Weigh
10	100	Dough Prep
	----	1st Rise
20		Shaping
5	120	Final Rise
10	70	Bake
5	30	Cool
70	320	TOTAL
1:10	5:20	6 hrs 30 min

Milan Italy during the time of the Roman Empire, is most often cited as the birthplace of the Panettone, or "large Cake. Its association with Christmas began in the middle ages when the serving of precious wheat bread was used to celebrate the holiday.

%	Ingredient	Volume	Grams	Volume	Grams
		4" size	240	6" size	480.0
40.36	Milk; whole	1/3C +1 1/2Tbs	96.77	3/4C +1Tbs	193.73
11.81	Unsalted Butter; pieces; room temp	2Tbs	28.35	1/4C	56.7
19.58	Eggs; room temp	1 large	47.0	2 large	94.0
7.88	Egg Yolk*	1 large	18.9	2 large	37.8
1.25	Salt	1/2tsp	3.0	1tsp	6.0
10.0	Granulated sugar	2Tbs	24.0	1/4C	48.0
100.0	Bread flour	2C	240.0	4C	480.0
0.83	Dried Orange peel**	1tsp	2.0	2tsp	4.0
0.28	Ground nutmeg	1/4tsp	0.67	1/2tsp	1.34
0.21	Cardamom	1/4tsp	0.5	1/2tsp	1.0
2.59	Rapid Rise Yeast	2tsp	6.22	4tsp	12.44
0.73	Anise seed	3/4tsp	1.75	1 1/2tsp	3.5
58.33	Mixed fruit; dried and candied citrus	1/2C +2Tbs	140.0	1C +1/4C	280.0
31.01	Raisins	1/2C	74.42	1C	148.83
284.86	TOTAL		683.58		1367.16
	Glaze				
	Caster Sugar	1Tbs		1Tbs	
	Milk	1Tbs		1Tbs	

Hydration = *(193.73g+94g+37.8g)/480g = 325.53g/480g = .6782 or 67.82%*

Holiday 75

*****Save egg white for optional egg wash.**
****If using fresh orange zest, double the weight.**

Preparation

- Be sure to review the formula, directions, and your machine's requirements before proceeding.
- Assemble and weigh/measure all ingredients. It will make your work much easier to have all weighed/measured and ready to follow directions.
- *Four to twelve hours before making, soak the raisins in your favorite liqueur; we prefer Grand Marnier, and soak for at least 4 hours.*
- Gently and safely warm cold eggs by placing whole eggs in a bowl and covering with moderately hot tap water for *10* minutes.
- Ensure milk at *room temperature*.
- Beat egg(s) & egg yolk(s).
- Melt/soften butter in microwave (be sure to cover with paper towel).
- For Glaze: Just before baking is complete, mix *1* tablespoon of milk with *1* tablespoon of caster sugar.
- Liquid Mix: Combine the milk, melted butter, beaten eggs & egg yolk, salt, and sugar in a medium (large if using by Hand) bowl, or use the bread pan fitted with the kneading paddle if utilizing the Bread Machine.
- Flour Mix: Combine flour, dried orange peel, ground nutmeg and cardamom.
- It takes six *16oz* (*453.4g*) containers of mixed fruit to make ten 6" loaves.
- It takes *3* containers to make ten 4" loaves.

Bread Machine

Yield: - The smaller size will yield one panettone for a *4"* diameter mould and the larger will yield two *4"* diameter panettones, or one *6"* diameter panettone.

- Place the Liquid Mix in the bread pan fitted with kneading paddle. Cover with the Flour Mix and make a shallow hole in the center and place in the yeast.

- Place the bread pan in the bread maker. Press *Menu* and select *Dough Cycle*. Select *1* lb (*240g* flour) or *2* lb (*480g* flour). Press *Start* to mix, knead, and rise. Total Time = *1:25* for *1* lb loaf; *1:40* for 2 lb loaf.

- When Mix-in signal sounds *(1 lb loaf = 1:12; 2 lb loaf = 1:19 Remaining)* add the Anise seeds, candied fruit and raisins. We have maximized the amount of candied fruit and raisins so you will need to assist the kneading with a spatula. If necessary, Pause the machine and then turn and mix the dough. I have found that it takes about *6-8* minutes of assisting until a ball (more or less) begins to form. We want the kneading paddle to continue turning over the dough to thoroughly mix all ingredients.

- When dough cycle is complete, remove dough and place onto a floured surface. Gently punch down. **Go to Continue All.**

Prep & Shape

- If you using the larger amount, leave alone to get a six inch loaf, otherwise, divide dough in half to get two *4"* loaves. Knead each for about a *minute*. Place in paper molds (no greasing required) or greased metal high molds (If you can't get proper Panettone Molds, use two *2* lb coffee cans). Optional; baste with melted butter.

- Cover and let rise in a warm place, free from drafts, *1 1/2 to 2* hours. Meanwhile, preheat oven to *350°F/176.7°C*.

Prep & Bake

- Uncover dough, cut a cross into the top and, if desired, baste with <u>egg white</u>.

- Bake at *350°F/176.7°C* for *20* minutes, then reduce temperature to *325°F/162.8°C* and bake for another *45-50* minutes (longer for *6"*). To prevent overbrowning, cover loaves with aluminum foil or parchment paper when the loaf reaches a shade of brown that you like.

- Remove when cake tester is removed without any sticky dough. Or, my preference, use your instant read thermometer and remove when it reads *195°F/90.6°C – 205°F/96.1°C*. Place on wire rack and if desired, brush with <u>sugar glaze</u>.

Notes

Christmas Stollen

> Use the glaze or just sprinkle with confectioner's sugar. We like soaking the fruit in Grand Marnier liquor while others may prefer dark rum.

Adapted From "A Taste of Home"[28]

%	Ingredient	Volume	Grams	Volume	Grams
			270.0		**540.0**
44.44	Milk	1/2C	120.0	1C	240.0
0.26	Almond Extract	1/4tsp	0.7	1/2tsp	1.4
17.41	Large eggs	1	47.0	2	94.0
21.0	Unsalted Butter; melted	1/4C	56.7	1/2C	113.4
8.89	Granulated Sugar	2Tbs	24.0	1/4C	48.0
1.11	Salt	1/2tsp	3.0	1tsp	6.0
100.0	All Purpose flour	2 1/4C	270.0	4 1/2C	540.0
2.22	Dried Orange Peel	1Tbs	6.0	2Tbs	12.0
1.30	Dried Lemon Peel	1/2Tbs	3.5	1Tbs	7.0
0.24	Ground Cinnamon	1/4tsp	.65	1/2tsp	1.3
0.24	Ground Nutmeg	1/4tsp	.65	1/2tsp	1.3
2.63	Rapid rise yeast	2 1/4tsp	7.09	4 1/2tsp	14.18
20.67	Raisins	1/3C+2 1/2tsp	55.81	3/4C	111.62
20.83	Mixed Candied Fruit	1/4C	56.25	1/2C	112.5
8.89	Dried Currants	2Tbs	24.0	1/4C	48.0
6.94	Almonds; Slivered	1/4C	18.75	1/2C	37.5
257.07	**Total**	**Total**	**692.8**	**Total**	**1385.6**
	OPTIONAL				
	Rum/Grand M./Orange juice	1/3C+1Tbs	90.0	3/4C	180.0
	GLAZE				
	Confection Sugar	1/2C	52.0	1C	104.0
	Milk	2Tbs	30.0	1/4C	60.0

Hydration = (240g+94g)/540g = 334g/540g = .6185 or 61.85%

---

[28] "German Stollen Recipe," *tasteofhome.com*, Last Accessed 11/10/2017, http://www.tasteofhome.com/recipes/german-stollen

Preparation

Bread Machine		
A	P	Action
5		Preparation
15		Assemble & Weigh
10	100	Dough Prep
	----	1st Rise
20	10	Shaping
	30	Final Rise
5	30	Bake
5	30	Cool
60	200	TOTAL
1:00	3:20	4 hrs 20 min

Be sure to review the recipe, and your machine's requirements before proceeding.
- Assemble and weigh/measure all ingredients. It will make your work much easier to have all weighed/measured and ready to follow directions.
- <u>Soak</u>: One or more of the fruit should be presoaked in the rum/grand M./orange juice for at least several hours.
- Melt the <u>butter</u> in the microwave.
- Ensure <u>Milk</u> at *80°F/26.7°C – 90°F/32.2°C*.
- Beat the eggs.

- <u>Liquid Mix</u>: Put <u>milk</u>, <u>almond extract</u>, <u>beaten eggs</u>, <u>melted butter</u>, <u>sugar</u>, and <u>salt</u> in a large bowl and mix thoroughly, or use the bread pan fitted with the kneading paddle if utilizing the Bread Machine.
- <u>Flour Mix</u>: In a medium bowl, add the <u>flour</u>, <u>grated orange peel</u>, <u>grated lemon peel</u>, <u>ground cinnamon</u> and <u>ground nutmeg</u>. Mix together.

Bread Machine

- Place the <u>Liquid Mix</u> in the bread pan fitted with kneading paddle and then cover with the <u>Flour Mix</u>. Make a shallow hole in the center and put in the <u>yeast</u>.

- Place the bread pan in the bread maker. Press *Menu* and select *Dough Cycle*. Select *1* lb (*270g* flour) or *2* lb (*540g* flour). Press *Start* to mix, knead, and rise. Total Time = *1:25* for *1* lb loaf; *1:40* for *2* lb loaf.

- When the Mix-in Signal sounds *(1 lb loaf = 1:12; 2 lb loaf = 1:19 Remaining)* add the <u>raisins</u>, <u>mixed candied fruit</u>, <u>dried currants</u> and <u>slivered almonds</u>.

- At end of the dough cycle, remove dough and place on a floured work surface. Gently punch down. Turn off the machine.

Prep & Shape

- Preheat oven to *375°F/190.6°C*.

- If doing two loaves, divide in half; let rest for *10* minutes; roll each half into a *12* inch x *8* inch oval. Fold one the long sides over to within *1* inch of the opposite

80 Delicious Direct Breads

side; press edges lightly to seal. Place on parchment lined baking sheet. Cover and let rise until almost doubled; about *30* minutes.

Bake

- Reduce temperature and bake at *350°F/176.7°C* for *25-30* minutes or until golden brown. Cool on wire racks. Dust with confectioner's sugar or combine glaze ingredients and drizzle over loaves.

Notes

Italian

Calzone

Bread Machine		
A	P	Action
5		Preparation
15		Assemble & Weigh
5	10	Dough Prep
	60	1st Rise
20	20	Shaping
20		Filling
5	20	Bake
5	0	Cool
75	110	TOTAL
1:15	1:50	3 hrs 5 min

{ Developed in Naples, Italy, it is a baked "folded over pizza" stuffed with your choice of meats and cheeses. }

%	Ingredient	Volume	Grams	Volume	Grams
		Small	**250.0**	Regular	**500.0**
56.6	Water; 80-90F	5/8 C	141.75	1 1/4 C	283.0
0.8	Granulated sugar	1/2 tsp	2.0	1 tsp	4.0
2.4	Salt	1 tsp	6.0	2 tsp	12.0
6.0	Extra virgin olive oil	1 Tbs	15.0	2 Tbs	30.0
100	Unbleached white bread flour	2 1/8 C	250.0	4 1/8 C	500.0
0.93	Rapid rise yeast	3/4 tsp	2.33	1 1/2 tsp	4.67
166.73	TOTAL		411.08		822.17

Hydration = *283g/500g = .566 or 56.6%*

- This formula is set up to allow for preparing the dough on one day, and then prepare and bake the calzone the next day.
- Flexibility: Keep in mind that the "interior" of the calzone is yours to design. Put whatever you want in there.

Preparation

- Be sure to review the recipe, and your machine's requirements before proceeding.
- Assemble and weigh/measure all ingredients. It will make your work much easier to have all weighed/measured and ready to follow directions.

- <u>Liquid Mix</u>: Mix <u>water</u>, <u>sugar</u>, <u>olive oil</u>, and <u>salt</u> in a medium (large if mixing by Hand) bowl, or use the bread pan fitted with the kneading paddle if utilizing the Bread Machine.

Bread Machine

- Place the <u>Liquid Mix</u> in the bread pan fitted with kneading paddle and then cover with the <u>flour</u>. Make a shallow hole in the center and put in the <u>yeast</u>.

- Place the bread pan in the bread maker. Press *Menu* and select *Dough Cycle*. Select *1* lb (*250g* flour) or *2* lb (*500g* flour). Press *Start* to mix, knead, and rise. You will NOT be using full cycle. You will run the machine about *10-11* minutes to achieve a dough temperature less than *80F*. Check temperature to ensure that it between *75°F/23.9°C – 80°F/26.7°C*.

- When Desired Dough Temperature (*DDT*) is reached, either leave it in the bread machine (you may want to remove the kneading paddle). or remove dough and place onto a floured surface. If removing, place it in a clean oiled bowl, and cover with plastic wrap. *In either case, leave dough to rise until double in bulk (about 1 hour).*

FILLING	US	Metric gram	US	Metric gram
Prosciutto; cut into 1-inch chunks	1/3 lb	151.0	2/3 lb	302.0
Mozzarella cheese; cubed	1/2 lb	227.0	1 lb	454.0
Freshly grated parmesan cheese	1/4 C	25.0	1/2 C	50.0
Ricotta cheese	1/2 C	113.0	1 C	226.0
Chopped Fresh Basil	1 Tb	0.88	2 Tb	1.75
Egg; large	1	-	2	-
Spinach; Mushrooms; To taste	---	---	---	---
black pepper & garlic salt; to taste	---	---	---	---
Topping & Dip				
Large egg	1	-	1	-
Marinara Sauce: for dipping	---	---	---	---

- Lightly oil a large baking sheet, or line it with parchment paper.

Prep & Shape

- Preheat oven to *425°F/218.3°C* at least *45* minutes before baking.

-Divide the dough into two (or four) equal pieces. If you have followed the formula table, each dough ball should weigh out at about *200* grams. Shape dough into balls; let rest *20* minutes. Roll out each piece of dough into a flat round, about *1/4* inch thick.

- In an appropriate sized bowl, mix together beaten <u>egg</u> , <u>cheeses</u>, <u>basil</u>, and use <u>garlic salt</u> & <u>black pepper</u> to taste. Add <u>meat(s)</u>, <u>spinach</u>, and <u>mushrooms</u> after spreading the mix on half of the dough.

- Divide the filling between the pieces of dough, placing it on half only. Leave a *1/2* inch border all around.

- Dampen the edges of each dough round with <u>water</u>, fold the remaining dough over the filling then crimp the edges of each calzone with your fingers to seal securely.

Prep & Bake

- Place the calzone on the baking sheet lined with parchment paper, brush tops with <u>olive oil</u>. If desired, cover with plastic wrap and place in the refrigerator for up to two hours.

- When ready, bake at *425°F/218.3°C* for *20* minutes, or until golden and well risen.

- Serve hot with <u>marinara sauce</u> on the side.

Notes

Classic Italian Loaf

> Great bread! Open crumb, and light and slightly chewy. Crust is light and soft as it should be as this is not a French bread with its typical crispy crust.

Bread Machine		
A	P	Action
5		Preparation
15		Assemble & Weigh
5	100	Dough Prep
	----	1st Rise
20		Shaping
	60	Final Rise
10	35	Bake
5	30	Cool
55	225	TOTAL
1:00	3:45	4 hrs 45 min

%	Ingredient	Volume	Grams	Volume	Grams
			250.0		**500.0**
60.48	Water	2/3C	151.2	1 1/3C	302.4
1.5	Extra virgin olive oil	3/4tsp	3.75	1 1/2tsp	7.5
2.66	Light brown sugar	1/2Tb	6.65	1Tb	13.29
1.8	Salt	3/4tsp	4.5	1 1/2tsp	9.0
100.0	Unbleached white bread flour	2C+1Tb+1tsp	250.0	4C+2Tb+2tsp	500.0
1.4	Rapid rise yeast	1 1/8 tsp	3.5	2 1/4tsp	7.0
167.84	**TOTAL**		**419.60**		**839.19**
	For the Wash				
	Egg	1/2 whole	26.5	1 Whole	47
	Water	1/2 Tb	7.4	1Tb	14.8

Hydration = 302.4g/500g = .6048 or 60.48%

Preparation

- Be sure to review the recipe, and your machine's requirements before proceeding.
- Assemble and weigh/measure all ingredients. It will make your work much easier to have all weighed/measured and ready to follow directions.
- Ensure <u>water</u> at *105°F/40.6°C – 115°F/46.1°C.*
- <u>Liquid Mix</u>: Mix <u>water</u>, <u>olive oil</u>, <u>sugar</u>, and <u>salt</u> in medium (large if mixing by Hand) bowl, or use the bread pan fitted with the kneading paddle if utilizing the Bread Machine.

88 Delicious Direct Breads

Bread Machine

- Place the <u>Liquid Mix</u> in the bread pan fitted with kneading paddle and then cover with the <u>flour</u>. Make a shallow hole in the center and put in the <u>yeast</u>.

- Place the bread pan in the bread maker. Press *Menu* and select *Dough Cycle*. Select *1* lb (*250g* flour) or *2* lb (*500g* flour). Press *Start* to mix, knead, and rise. Total Time = *1:25* for *1* lb loaf; *1:40* for *2* lb loaf.

- When dough cycle is complete, remove dough and place onto a floured surface. ***Go to Continue All.***

Prep & Shape

- Form into desired shape (first divide dough into two pieces if using larger formula) Place the loaves seam side down on a baking sheet generously sprinkled with cornmeal (or use parchment paper). Place loaves in a warm place, and let rise for *60* minutes, or until double in size. Meanwhile, preheat oven to *375°F/190.6°C*.

Prep & Bake

- In a small bowl, beat together <u>egg</u> and <u>*1* tablespoon water</u>. Brush the loaves with <u>egg mixture</u>. Make a single long, quick cut down the center of the loaves with a sharp knife.

- Bake at *375°F/190.6°C* for *30 to 35* minutes, or until loaves sound hollow when tapped on the bottom (about *205°F/96.1°C*).

- Place on wire rack to cool. Best taste and flavor after *30 - 60* min of cooling.

Notes

Muffuletta Bread

Bread Machine		
A	P	Action
5		Preparation
15		Assemble & Weigh
5	35	Dough Prep
	60	1st Rise
20	20	Shaping
	60	Final Rise
10	20	Bake
5	30	Cool
55	225	TOTAL
1:00	3:45	4 hrs 40 min

The bread is an Italian round loaf (from *8 - 14* inches) that forms the basis for a Sicilian sandwich creation that includes Italian meats, cheeses and a olive salad that makes it truly distinctive.

%	Ingredient	Volume	Grams	Volume	Grams
			375.0		*750.0*
56.0	Water	3/4C+2Tb+2 1/2tsp	210.0	1C+3/4C+2Tb	420.0
4.0	Extra virgin olive oil	1Tbs	15.0	2Tb	30.0
0.8	Salt	1/2tsp	3.0	1tsp	6.0
1.07	Granulated sugar	1tsp	4.0	2tsp	8.0
100	Unbleached white bread flour	3C+2Tbs	375.0	6C+1/4C	750.0
0.83	Rapid rise yeast	1tsp	3.11	2tsp	6.22
162.7	TOTAL		610.11		1220.22
	Sesame Seeds	Coating		Coating	
	1 Egg White; Beaten	Egg Wash		Egg Wash	

Hydration = *420g/750g = .56 or 56.0%*

Muffuletta bread is an Italian round loaf that is about *1 1/2* inches high, with a diameter of *8* to *14* inches. We could not find any specific formula, with only the general aspects of a "round Italian loaf" being given.

Preparation

- <u>Liquid Mix</u>: Mix the <u>water</u>, <u>olive oil</u>, <u>salt</u> and <u>sugar</u> in a medium (large if mixing by Hand) bowl, or use the bread pan fitted with the kneading paddle if utilizing the Bread Machine.

Italian 91

Bread Machine
- Place Liquid Mix in the bread pan fitted with the kneading paddle. Cover with the flour, and make a shallow indent in the center and add the yeast. This is a low hydration bread, and the dough will be stiff, dry and initially shaggy. I often aid the mixing and kneading by pausing the machine and using one had to mix and knead in the machine.

- Place the bread pan in the machine; Press *Menu* and select *Dough Cycle*.

- **For *375g* of flour**, press *Loaf* and select *1* lb. Press *Start* to begin mixing and kneading *(1:25 Total Time)*. You may need to assist the mixing/kneading as this is a *firm & tight* dough (low hydration). Place machine on *PAUSE* and then use one hand to mix and squish the dough in the early stage of coming together.

- Remove from machine when cycle is complete and scrape dough on to a greased or floured work surface. **Go To Prep & Shape.**

- **For *750g* of flour**, press *Loaf* and select *2* lb. Press *Start* to begin mixing and kneading *(1:40 Total Time)*. We will NOT be using full cycle as there is too much flour in this formula. Let it mix and knead and then remove before the first machine rise (*35* minutes elapsed time; *1:05* on the machine).

- Place dough on a floured work surface and shape into a ball. Place in an oiled bowl, and turn to coat all surface area. Cover with plastic wrap and place in a warm place to rise for *45-60* minutes, or until double in size. Gently punch down and turn out onto a floured work surface.

Prep & Shape
Shape into a flat round (about *7* inches) and let rest for *20* minutes. Expand flat shape to about *12* inches.

- Place into a well oiled *12* inch cast iron pan. Lightly spritz with water (or brush with a little olive oil) and sprinkle with sesame seeds. Gently push seeds into the dough. Cover and let rise in a warm place for about *1* hour. In the meantime, preheat the oven to *450°F/232.2°C*.

Prep & Bake

- Beat <u>*1 egg white*</u> with <u>*1 Tablespoon of water*</u>. Just before placing dough in the oven, brush the top with the <u>egg wash</u>. Place in the oven and reduce temperature to *425°F/218.3°C*. Bake for *18-22* minutes until crust is golden brown and crispy.

- Remove from oven, place on pot holders (or other safe surface) and carefully remove the bread from pan by turning pan at an angle and using a spatula, assist the bread to the wire rack. Let cool uncovered.

Muffuletta Sandwich

The bread is an Italian round loaf (from *8 - 14* inches) that forms the basis for a Sicilian sandwich creation that includes Italian meats, cheeses and a olive salad that makes it truly distinctive. Although several locations (and recipes on the Internet) heat the sandwiches, we were told that a Muffuletta is never toasted or baked; it must always be served cold.

Muffuletta		
A	P	Action
15		Assemble & Weigh
40		Olive Salad Prep
20		Preparation
75		TOTAL
1:15	0:00	1 hrs 15 min

New Orleans is the home of *Muffuletta*, with the delicatessen owner of "Central Grocery" claiming to have invented it in *1906*. Lupo Salvatore said he started making Muffulettas for the men working in the nearby French Market and on the docks. Marie Lupo Tusa, daughter of the Central Grocery's founder, tells the story of the sandwich's origin in her *1980* cookbook, <u>Marie's Melting Pot</u>:[29]

> One of the most interesting aspects of my father's grocery is his unique creation, the Muffuletta sandwich. The Muffuletta was created in the early *1900's* when the Farmers' Market was in the same area as the grocery. Most of the farmers who sold their produce there were Sicilian. Every day they used to come of my father's grocery for lunch.
>
> They would order some salami, some ham, a piece of cheese, a little olive salad, and either long braided Italian bread or round muffuletta bread. In typical Sicilian fashion they ate everything separately. The farmers used to sit on crates or barrels and try to eat while precariously balancing their small trays covered with food on their knees. My father suggested that it would be easier for the farmers if he cut the bread and put everything on

---

[29] Marie Lupo Tusa, *Marie's Melting Pot*. ISBN 0960706291, T & M Pubns, 1980.

Italian 93

it like a sandwich; even if it was not typical Sicilian fashion. He experimented and found that the thicker, braided Italian bread was too hard to bite but the softer round muffuletta was ideal for his sandwich. In very little time, the farmers came to merely ask for a "muffuletta" for their lunch.

Olive Salad*

- 1 (1-quart) jar mixed pickled vegetables**
- 1 red onion
- 1 (16-ounce) jar pitted green olives
- 2 (2 1/4-ounce) cans chopped ripe olives
- 1 (7.25-ounce) jar roasted red peppers
- 1/2 cup Kalamata Olives; pitted
- 1/4 cup chopped pepperoncini peppers
- 2 tablespoons capers
- 1 tablespoon minced garlic
- 1/2 cup olive oil
- 1 1/2 teaspoons dried parsley flakes
- 1 teaspoon dried oregano
- 1 teaspoon dried basil
- 1/2 teaspoon ground black pepper
- Green olive brine; *1/4 - 1/2* cup

* If you want your sandwich a bit "hotter," add some crushed red pepper flakes.
** Use mixed pickled vegetables that contain cauliflower, onion, carrot, pepper, and celery.

The following is a *modification* of a Southern Living Recipe first presented in July *1998*[30]

Ingredients

- 2 cups Olive Salad
- 1 (12-inch) round Italian loaf, split horizontally
- 1/2 pound sliced hard salami
- 1/2 lb Mortadella
- 1/2 pound sliced cooked ham
- 14 thin provolone cheese slices

---

[30] "Olive Salad," *myrecipes.com*, Last Accessed 11/10/2017, http://www.myrecipes.com/recipe/olive-salad-10000000522564/

TKB Note: For 10 inch round loaf: use 1/3 lb. and for 14 inch use 3/4 lb.

Preparation

Drizzle the cut side of both rounds lightly with olive oil or garlic oil, then spread the olive salad onto the bottom round. Layer on the ham, salami, provolone, mortadella, and provolone cheese slices. Cover with the top piece of bread. Cut crosswise into sandwiches.

We don't use a food processor; could result in over chopping; you don't get clean cuts; don't like the way it looks. In other words, it's better done by hand.

- Drain pickled vegetables, discarding the liquid.
- Drain pitted green olives, reserving the liquid.
- Drain chopped ripe olives; discarding the liquid.
- Drain roasted red peppers; discarding the liquid
- Coarsely chop pickled vegetables, red onion, pitted green olives, pitted Kalamata olives, roasted red peppers, and pepperoncini peppers.
- In a medium sized bowl, stir (Combine) capers, minced garlic, olive oil, parsley flakes, dried oregano, dried basil, and black pepper with the chopped vegetables.
- Add reserved green olive brine to taste. We suggest starting out with no more than *1/4* cup.
- Place in a sealed container and refrigerate overnight

Notes

Sausage Bread

> This is the recipe that really got us back into bread making. It's also a wonderful loaf without the sausage.

Bread Machine		
A	P	Action
5		Preparation
30		Assemble & Weigh
5	100	Dough Prep
	----	1st Rise
20	10	Shaping
	60	Final Rise
5	30	Bake
5	60	Cool
70	260	TOTAL
1:10	4:20	5 hrs 30 min

Inspired by Aunt Jackie & Uncle Junior.

%	Ingredient	Volume	Grams	Volume	Grams
			250.0		**500.0**
65.0	Water	2/3C+ 2 1/4tsp	162.5	1 1/3C+1Tbs+ 1 1/2tsp	325.0
6.0	Extra virgin olive oil	1Tbs	15.0	2Tbs	30.0
2.17	Sea salt	3/4+1/8tsp	5.43	1+1/2+1/8tsp	10.85
0.80	Granulated sugar	1/2tsp	2.0	1tsp	4.0
100.0	Unbleached white bread flour	2C+1Tbs+1tsp	250.0	4C+2Tbs+2tsp	500.0
4.0	Wheat bran unprocessed coarse	1/4C	10.0	1/2C	20.0
1.5	Rapid rise yeast	1 1/4tsp	3.75	2 1/2tsp	7.5
87.57	Italian Ground sausage; browned	1/2 lb	226.8	1 lb	453.59
267.04	**TOTAL**		**675.48**		**1350.96**
	Sesame or poppy seeds; optional				
	Corn meal; for dusting				
	1 egg for the wash				

Hydration = *325g/500g = .65 or 65.0%*

Italian 97

Preparation
- Be sure to review your machine's requirements/limitations before proceeding.
- Assemble and weigh/measure all ingredients. It will make your work much easier to have all weighed/measured and ready to follow directions.
- Brown the *1* pound (or *1/2* lb) of sausage, drain fat and place on paper towels.
- If making one loaf, use all the dough. If making two loaves, separate into two equal amounts and shape into loaves.
- Beat together: *1* egg and *1* Tbs of water; put aside for glazing loaves.
- Ensure Water at *80°F/26.7°C – 90°F/32.2°C*.
- Liquid Mix: Mix water, olive oil, salt, and sugar in a medium (large if mixing by Hand) bowl, or use the bread pan fitted with the kneading paddle if utilizing the Bread Machine.
- Flour Mix: the flour and wheat bran together.

Bread Machine
- Place Liquid Mix in the bread pan fitted with the kneading paddle. Cover with the Flour Mix and make a shallow hole in the center and place in the yeast.

- Place the bread pan in the bread maker. Press *Menu* and select *Dough Cycle*. Select *1* lb (*250g* flour) or *2* lb (*500g* flour). Press *Start* to mix, knead, and rise. Total Time = *1:25* for *1* lb loaf; *1:40* for *2* lb loaf.

- At the end of the Dough Cycle, remove dough and kneading paddle. Turn off/unplug bread machine. Turn the dough out on a floured surface.

Prep & Shape
- For one loaf use all, or for two, divide into two equal parts. Let both "rest" *10* minutes. Flatten each part with a rolling pin to about *1/8* inch in thickness. Add sausage evenly over flattened dough. Roll up each sheet of dough tightly to make a long slender loaf. Press firmly along the rolled edges and ends to seal.

- Sprinkle baking sheet with Corn Meal or use banneton and sprinkle with flour, or use baking sheet lined with parchment paper. Put the loaves on the sheets, leaving enough space between them so that they will be crusty on all sides. (Option: Use baguette cooking trays).

- Let rise uncovered until double in bulk (about *45-60* minutes). Meanwhile, prepare oven for *Hearth Baking*, and preheat to *475°F/246.1°C*. Note we start with this higher heat because of the heat loss from opening the door, even for a short time.

Prep & Bake

When dough is ready, cut diagonal gashes in the loaves with an oiled sharp knife or razor, enough to cut through just one layer. Brush egg white mixture (egg wash) over the top of the loaves (this will give a shiny golden crust) . Sprinkle with Sesame or poppy seeds.

- Place in preheated oven and then put in cup of ice cubes in the cast iron pan, close the oven door and reduce temperature to *450°F/232.2°C*.

- Bake for *5* minutes then reduce heat to *425°F/218.3°C*. Spritz oven with water *2* or three times to keep up some steam.

- After a total of *15* minutes, remove from the oven and brush again with the egg wash. Return bread to the oven, remove cast iron pan with water and reduce the heat to *375°F/190.6°C*, and bake until the bread sounds hollow when you tap it (about another *10-15* minutes; *200°F/93.3°C – 210°F/98.9°C* at sea level).

- Cool on a rack. Best taste and flavor after *60* min of cooling.

Notes

Stromboli

Bread Machine		
A	P	Action
5		Preparation
15		Assemble & Weigh
5	100	Dough Prep
	----	1st Rise
25	5	Shaping
	30	Final Rise
5	35	Bake
5	0	Cool
55	170	TOTAL
0:55	1:50	2 hrs 50 min

Dough is flattened, and covered with cheeses and Italian cold cuts (salami, pepperoni, ham, sausage, etc.) and then rolled up like a jelly roll, and baked to perfection. Have some fun and look up why it was named after a 1950's movie. *Compare with a Calzone.*

%	Ingredient	Volume	Grams	Volume	Grams
		Small	**250.0**	Regular	**500.0**
56.6	Water; 80-90F	5/8 C	141.75	1 1/4 C	283.0
0.8	Granulated sugar	1/2 tsp	2.0	1 tsp	4.0
2.4	Salt	1 tsp	6.0	2 tsp	12.0
6.0	Extra virgin olive oil	1 Tbs	15.0	2 Tbs	30.0
100	Unbleached white bread flour	2 1/8 C	250.0	4 1/8 C	500.0
0.93	Rapid rise yeast	3/4 tsp	2.33	1 1/2 tsp	4.67
166.73	TOTAL		411.08		822.17

Hydration = *283g/500g = .566 or 56.6%*

Preparation
- Be sure to review your machine's requirements/limitations before proceeding.
- Assemble and weigh/measure all ingredients. It will make your work much easier to have all weighed/measured and ready to follow directions.
- <u>Liquid Mix</u>: Mix <u>water</u>, <u>sugar</u>, <u>olive oil</u>, and <u>salt</u> in a medium (large if mixing by Hand) bowl, or use the bread pan fitted with the kneading paddle if utilizing the Bread Machine.

Bread Machine
- Place the <u>Liquid Mix</u> in the bread pan fitted with kneading paddle and then cover with the <u>flour</u>. Make a shallow hole in the center and put in the <u>yeast</u>.

Italian 101

- Place the bread pan in the bread maker. Press *Menu* and select *Dough Cycle*. Select *1* lb (*250*g flour) or *2* lb (*500*g flour). Press *Start* to mix, knead, and rise. Total Time = *1:25* for *1* lb loaf; *1:40* for *2* lb loaf.

- When the dough cycle is complete, remove dough and place onto a floured surface and gently punch down.

Prep & Shape

- Lightly oil a baking sheet(s). Divide dough in half for *Small* size, and into *4* equal pieces if using *Regular* size.

Adapted From Guy Fieri[31]

	Small			*Regular*		
FOR THE FILLING	*Volume*	*oz*	*grams*	*Volume*	*oz*	*grams*
Unsalted butter; melted	3 Tb	1.5	42.53	6 Tb	3.0	85.06
Garlic clove; minced	1 whole	0.18	5.0	2 whole	0.36	10.0
Parmesan; grated plus extra for the tops	1/2 C	1.75	49.61	1 C	3.5	99.22
Salami*		5.0	142.5		10	285.0
Deli ham*		5.0	142.5		10	285.0
Bresaola*		5.0	142.5		10	285.0
Mozzarella*		~5.0	1~42.5		~10	~285.0
Pepper jack*		~5.0	~142.5		~10	~285.0
Fresh basil leaves; finely sliced	~1/4 C	~0.12	~3.5	~1/2 C	~0.24	~7.0
Black pepper; freshly ground	To taste			To taste		
Marinara Sauce of your choosing	For Dipping			For Dipping		

* thinly sliced

---

[31] Guy Fieri "Stromboli," *foodnetwork.com*, Last Accessed 11/10/2017, http://www.foodnetwork.com/recipes/guy-fieri/stromboli-recipe-2124726

Small: Serves Two

- Divide the dough in half and, working with one piece at a time, stretch the dough into a *8-by-12*-inch rectangle. Arrange the dough rectangle so the *12*-inch-long side is closest to you. Brush the surface with half of the melted butter, then spread the minced garlic out evenly over the top, remembering to split the filling ingredient quantities evenly across both Stromboli. Leave a *1*-inch border around the far and side borders.

- Sprinkle the dough with the parmesan, then layer with the salami slices. Top the salami with a layer of deli ham and then a layer of bresaola. Shingle the cheese slices over the top and finish with fresh basil and some ground black pepper. With the covered edge closest to you, roll the dough up into a log, gently sealing the ends of the roll as you go. When you get to the end that has no filling on it, gently press to seal, then place the roll seam-side down on a nonstick sheet tray or a parchment lined baking sheet. Repeat the process with second piece of dough.

Regular: Serves Four
Repeat above if using Regular (or double dough size) recipe.

Small & Regular
Brush the tops of the dough with the remaining melted butter and sprinkle with parmesan. Bake at *375°F/190.5°C* in the center of the oven until golden brown and puffy, *25* to *30* minutes.

- Allow the Stromboli to cool *5* minutes before slicing it into thick slices with a serrated knife. Serve with the Marinara Sauce on the side or some mustard.

Notes

Rolls

Butter Rolls

{ Light, buttery, tender, and simply delicious. These are the perfect size for dinner rolls. }

Bread Machine		
A	P	Action
5		Preparation
15		Assemble & Weigh
5	35	Dough Prep
	60	1st Rise
15		Shaping
	60	Final Rise
10	20	Bake
5	30	Cool
55	205	TOTAL
0:55	3:25	4 hrs 20 min

Adapted From Southern Living[32]

%	Ingredient	Volume	Grams	Volume	Grams
		24 Rolls	**300.0**	*48 Rolls*	**600.0**
40.0	Milk	1/2 C	120.0	1 C	240.0
15.67	Large egg	1	47.0	2	94.0
18.9	Butter	1/4 C	56.7	1/2 C	113.4
2.5	Salt	1 1/4 tsp	7.5	2 1/2 tsp	15.0
16.0	Granulated sugar	1/4 C	48.0	1/2 C	96.0
100.0	All-purpose flour	2 1/2 C	300.0	5 C	600.0
2.33	Rapid rise yeast	2 1/4 tsp	7.0	4 1/2 tsp	14.0
195.4	**TOTAL**		**586.2**		**1172.4**
	Topping & Wash				
	Water	1 Tb	14.18	2 Tb	28.35
	Large egg	1	47.0	1	47.0
	Sesame or poppy seeds	Dusting			

Hydration = (240g+94g)/600g = 334g/600 = .5567 or 55.67%

Preparation

- Ensure <u>Milk</u> at *80°F/26.7°C – 90°F/32.2°C*.
- <u>Liquid Mix</u>: Add <u>milk</u>, <u>beaten egg(s)</u>, <u>melted butter</u>, <u>salt</u>, and <u>sugar</u> together in an appropriately sized bowl.

---

[32] *Southern Living 2000 Annual Recipes*. (Birmingham: Oxmoor House, Inc. Book Division of Southern Progress Corporation, 2000), 257.

Bread Machine
Place the <u>Liquid Mix</u> in the bread pan fitted with kneading paddle and then cover with the <u>flour</u>. Make a shallow hole in the center and put in the <u>yeast</u>.

- Place the bread pan in the bread maker. Press *Menu* and select *Dough Cycle*. Select *1* lb (*300g* flour) or *2* lb (*600g* flour). Press *Start* to mix, knead, and rise. Total Time = *1:25* for *1* lb loaf; *1:40* for *2* lb loaf.

- About *10* minutes before the end of the kneading cycle, examine the dough's consistency; it should be quite stiff, but not at all "gnarly;" adjust its consistency with additional flour or water, as necessary (This has been tested many times, and it is unlikely to need adjustment).

- When cycle is complete, transfer the dough to a lightly greased/floured work surface. Turn off the machine.

Prep & Shape
- If making *48* rolls, divided dough in half, and do the following twice.

- For *24* rolls: gently punch down and divide into *4* pieces. divide and shape each piece into *6* balls.

- Place on baking sheet lined with parchment paper. Cover with oiled plastic wrap and let rise for *1* hour. Meanwhile, preheat oven to *375°F/190.6°C*.

Prep & Bake
- Beat <u>egg</u> and <u>water</u> and brush over rolls and sprinkle with <u>sesame</u> or <u>poppy seeds</u>.

- Bake at *375°F/190.6°C* for *15* to *20* minutes or until golden brown.

- Remove from the oven, and cool on a wire rack.

Notes

Kaiser Rolls

Bread Machine		
A	P	Action
5		Preparation
15		Assemble & Weigh
5	35	Dough Prep
	60	1st Rise
20		Shaping
	60	Final Rise
10	18	Bake
5	30	Cool
60	203	TOTAL
1:00	3:23	4 hrs 23 min

We grew up on Long Island, NY, and "Deli" Kaiser Rolls were almost a daily occurrence. This recipe brings back the memories.

These deli-style "bulky rolls" are perfect for over-stuffed sandwiches. Top them with sesame or poppy seeds for that authentic "bakery look"

Adapted From: King Arthur Flour[33]

%	Ingredient	Volume	Grams	Volume	Grams
			360.0		**720.0**
45.0	Water	2/3C+2tsp	162.0	1 1/3C+1Tbs+ 1 1/2tsp	324.0
13.06	Egg	1 large	47.0	2 large	94.0
1.67	Granulated sugar	1 1/2tsp	6.0	2 1/2tsp	12.0
2.0	Salt	1 1/4tsp	7.2	2 1/2tsp	14.4
7.88	Unsalted butter	2Tbs	28.35	4Tbs	56.7
50.0	Unbleached All Purpose flour	1 1/2C	180.0	3C	360.0
50.0	Unbleached Bread Flour	1 1/2C	180.0	3C	360.0
1.25	Rapid rise yeast	1 1/2tsp	4.67	3tsp	9.34
170.86	TOTAL		615.22		1230.44
	Poppy & sesame seeds	Dusting		Dusting	

Hydration = (324g+94g)/(360g+360g) = 418g/720g = .5806 or 58.06%

360g of flour yields 6 (101.6g), 8 (76g), 12(51g) rolls
720g of flour yields 10 (122.5g), 12 (102g), 16 (76.8g), 24(50g) rolls

---

[33] "Kaiser Rolls," *kingarthurflour.com*, Last Accessed 11/10/2017, http://www.kingarthurflour.com/recipes/kaiser-rolls-recipe

Preparation

- Be sure to review the formula, and your machine's requirements before proceeding.
- Assemble and weigh/measure all ingredients. It will make your work much easier to have all weighed/measured and ready to follow directions.
- Ensure water at *85°F/29.4°C – 95°F/35°C.*
- Melt butter
- Beat egg
- Liquid Mix: Mix warm water, beaten egg, sugar, and salt in a medium (large if mixing by Hand) bowl, or use the bread pan fitted with the kneading paddle if utilizing the Bread Machine.
- Flour Mix: Combine the flours together

Bread Machine

Place the Liquid Mix in the bread pan fitted with kneading paddle and then cover with the Flour Mix. Make a shallow hole in the center and put in the yeast.

- Place the bread pan in the bread maker. Press *Menu* and select *Dough Cycle*. Select *1* lb (*360g* flour) or *2* lb (*720g* flour). Press *Start* to mix, knead, and rise. Total Time = *1:25* for *1* lb loaf; *1:40* for *2* lb loaf.

- About *10* minutes before the end of the kneading cycle, examine the dough's consistency; it should be quite stiff, but not at all "gnarly;" adjust its consistency with additional flour or water, as necessary (This has been tested many times, and it is unlikely to need adjustment).

- **For *360g* total flour**: When Cycle is complete, gently punch down dough and turn out on a floured work surface. Turn the bread machine off. ***Go To Prep & Shape.***

- **For *720g* total flour**: When mixing/kneading is done (*1:05* on timer), remove the dough from the bread pan and turn out on a floured surface. Turn the bread machine off. Remove the kneading paddle (if stuck into the dough) and shape the dough into a ball. Place in the oiled bowl (large enough to handle the doubling of the dough), and turn to coat all of the dough. Cover with plastic wrap and place in a warm place to rise for *45-60* minutes, or until just about double in bulk.

- When ready, gently punch down dough and turn out on a floured work surface.

Prep & Shape

- Shape into a hoagie roll or follow the following to create Kaiser rolls.

- Working with one ball of dough at a time, center your Kaiser stamp over the dough. Press down firmly, cutting almost to the bottom but not all the way through the dough. This is important; if you don't cut deeply enough, the shape disappears as the roll bakes; if you cut too deeply (all the way through), the roll will form "petals" as it rises and look like a daisy, not a Kaiser roll. Practice makes perfect! Repeat with the remaining rolls. Place the rolls cut-side down (this helps them retain their shape) onto a lightly greased or parchment-lined baking sheet (You may want to cover with poppy or sesame seeds before you place rolls face down on the baking sheet).

- Cover the rolls, and allow them to rise for *45 minutes to 1 hour*, or until they've almost doubled in volume. Meanwhile, prepare oven for *Hearth Baking*, and preheat to *475°F/246.1°C*.

Prep & Bake

- Turn the rolls cut-side up. If you haven't used poppy or sesame seeds prior, brush tops with milk (soft crust) or water (crispy crust) and coat with poppy or sesame seeds, if desired.

- Place in the preheated oven; put one cup ice cubes in the cast iron pan, and close the door. Reduce temperature to *425°F/218.3°C* and bake for *15 to 18* minutes, or until they're golden brown. Note: The use of steam (spraying water into the oven) creates a rustic and chewy crust. The use of an egg wash will result in a shinny golden crust.

- After *10-15* minutes of baking, remove cast iron pan filled with water and continue baking with dry heat.

- Remove them from the oven, and cool on a wire rack.

Notes

Norm's New York Style Onion Rolls[34]

> Norm is a retired New York City Baker who has responded to questions and provided suggestions and answers to many on the Internet I first came across Norm on *The Fresh Loaf* website while searching for "New York style onion rolls."

		FOR THE TOPPING			
%	Ingredient	Volume	Grams	Volume	Grams
	FOR THE TOPPING	6-10 Rolls	**400.0**	10-16	**800.0**
78.0	Water; reserve	1 1/3C+2tsp	312.0	2 3/4C	624.0
5.5	Dried minced onions	Scant 1/4C	22.0	Scant 1/2C	44.0
1.75	Vegetable oil	1/2Tbs	7.0	1Tbs	14.0
0.375	Salt	1/4tsp	1.5	1/2tsp	3.0
2.25	Poppy seeds	1Tbs	9.0	2Tbs	18.00
87.88	TOTAL		351.5		703.0
		FOR THE DOUGH			
%	Ingredient	Volume	Grams	Volume	Grams
		6-10 Rolls	**400.0**	10-16	**800.0**
	FOR THE DOUGH				
50.00	Water From Hydrating Onions	3/4C+2Tbs	200.0	1 3/4C	400.0
5.0	Vegetable oil	1Tbs+1tsp	20.0	2Tbs+2tsp	40.0
1.56	Salt	1tsp	6.24	2tsp	12.48
4.69	Sugar	1 1/2Tbs	18.76	3Tbs	37.52
4.0	Egg; beaten	1/3 large	16.0	2/3 large	32.0
100.00	Unbleached white bread flour	3 1/3C	400.0	6 2/3C	800.0
1.56	Diastatic Malt Powder	2 1/4tsp+1/8tsp	6.24	1Tbs+1 1/2tsp	12.48
1.54	Active dry yeast	2tsp	6.16	4tsp	12.32
168.35	TOTAL		670.4		1340.8

Hydration = (400g+32g)/800g = 432g/800g = .54 or 54.0%

---

[34] "Norm's Onion Rolls," thefreshloaf.com, Last Accessed 11/10/2017, http://www.thefreshloaf.com/recipes/normsonionrolls

400g of flour yields 6 (112g), 8 (84g), 10(67g), 12 (56g) rolls
800g of flour yields 10 (134g), 12 (112g), or 16 (84g), 24(56g) rolls

Bread Machine		
A	P	Action
5		Preparation
30		Assemble & Weigh
5	35	Dough Prep
	60	1st Rise
20	15	Shaping
	60	Final Rise
5	18	Bake
5	30	Cool
70	218	TOTAL
1:10	3:38	4 hrs 48 min

Topping

- Be sure to review the formula, and your machine's requirements before proceeding.
- Assemble and weigh/measure all ingredients. It will make your work much easier to have all weighed/measured and ready to follow directions.
- Soak the dried onions in *the* boiling water until fully hydrated (I leave them for *20-30* minutes). When hydrated, strain the onions and **save the water for later use**).
- Put the hydrated onions in a small bowl and add the salt, oil and poppy seeds; mix well. You can set it aside in the refrigerator until it is needed.

Dough Preparation

- Take the reserved hydrated onion water and remove enough water to equal *200.0/400.0* grams.
- Liquid Mix: Mix the appropriate amount of reserved hydrated onion water, vegetable oil, salt, sugar, and beaten egg in a medium (large if mixing by Hand) bowl, or use the bread pan fitted with the kneading paddle if utilizing the Bread Machine.
- Flour Mix: Combine the diastatic malt powder with the flour.

Bread Machine

- Place the Liquid Mix in the bread pan fitted with kneading paddle and then cover with the Flour Mix. Make a shallow hole in the center and put in the yeast.

- Place the bread pan in the bread maker. Press *Menu* and select *Dough Cycle*. Select *1* lb (*400g* flour) or *2* lb (*800g* flour). Press *Start* to mix, knead, and rise. Total Time = *1:25* for *1* lb loaf; *1:40* for *2* lb loaf.

- **For *400g* total flour**: When Cycle is complete, gently punch down dough and turn out on a floured work surface. Turn the bread machine off. ***Go To Prep & Shape.***

114 Delicious Direct Breads

- **For *800g* total flour**: When mixing/kneading is done (*1:05* on timer), remove the dough from the bread pan and turn out on a floured surface. Turn the bread machine off. Remove the kneading paddle (if stuck into the dough) and shape the dough into a ball. Place in the oiled bowl (large enough to handle the doubling of the dough), and turn to coat all of the dough. Cover with plastic wrap and place in a warm place to rise for *45- 60* minutes, or until just about double in bulk.

- When ready, gently punch down dough and turn out on a floured work surface.

Prep & Shape

- Divide dough into the desired number of equal pieces and make them into little dough balls, and cover with plastic wrap and let rest for *15* minutes.

- Sprinkle corn meal on a lightly greased, or parchment lined baking sheet.

- Dump the onion mix on your work surface and take the relaxed dough balls and turn them over into the onion mix and with the flat of your hand press them flat into the onion mix; about *1/4 to 1/2* inch thick. Put the rolls onion side up on the baking sheet with corn meal. Cover with lightly oiled plastic wrap, and proof until double in bulk (about *60* minutes). Meanwhile, prepare oven for *Hearth Baking*, and preheat to *475°F/246.1°C*.

Prep & Bake

- Just before putting them in the oven, press down the center of the roll with your thumb for a more authentic New York Onion Roll look.

- Place in the preheated oven, put one cup ice cubes in the cast iron pan, and close the door. Reduce temperature to *450°F/232.2°C* and bake for *12 to 18* minutes, or until they're golden brown. Remove them from the oven, and cool on a wire rack.

- In case you are wondering why we didn't remove the cast iron pan with water, it is simply due to the short baking time, and no real need to shift back to dry heat.

Unlike the Kaiser rolls, I wait for them to cool as the flavor is much better cooled than hot (Of course I was tempted and tried them hot once or twice; how else would I know this?).

Notes

Onion Buns

Whichever way you desire to shape and size them, they make delicious sandwich buns. These are second only to Kaiser rolls as a favorite for hamburgers.

Adapted From King Arthur Flour[35]

Bread Machine		
A	P	Action
5		Preparation
15		Assemble & Weigh
5	35	Dough Prep
5	60	1st Rise
20	15	Shaping
	60	Final Rise
5	25	Bake
5	30	Cool
60	225	TOTAL
1:00	3:45	4 hrs 45 min

%	Ingredient	Volume	Grams	Volume	Grams
			400.0		800.0
46.0	Lukewarm water	3/4C+1Tbs	184.0	1 1/2C+2Tbs	368.0
7.09	Unsalted butter; melted	2Tbs	28.35	4Tbs	56.7
11.75	Egg	1 large	47.0	2 large	94.0
11.0	Sugar	3Tbs+2tsp	44.0	1/3C+2Tbs	88.0
1.71	Salt	1 1/8tsp	6.84	2 1/4tsp	13.68
100.0	Unbleached bread flour	3 1/3C	400.0	6 2/3C	800.0
0.57	Onion powder	1 tsp	2.29	2tsp	4.58
2.33	Rapid rise yeast	1Tbs	9.33	2Tbs	18.66
4.5	Minced dried onion	3Tbs	18.0	1/4C+2Tbs	36.0
184.95	TOTAL		739.81		1479.62
	FOR THE TOPPING				
	Egg white	1Whole		2 Whole	
	Sesame, poppy, etc; optional				

Hydration = (368g+94g)/800g = 462g/800g = .5775 or 57.75%

400g of flour yields 6 (112g), 8 (91g), 10(73g), 12 (61g) rolls
800g of flour yields 12 (122g), or 16 (91.5g), 24(61g) rolls

---

[35] "Onion Buns, Published: 01/01/2010," *kingarthurflour.com*, Last Accessed 11/10/2017, http://www.kingarthurflour.com/recipes/onion-buns-recipe

Rolls 117

Preparation
Be sure to review the formula, and your machine's requirements before proceeding.
- Assemble and weigh/measure all ingredients. It will make your work much easier to have all weighed/measured and ready to follow directions.
- Ensure Water at *80°F/26.7°C – 90°F/32.2°C*.
- Beat egg and melt butter in microwave.
- Liquid Mix: Mix lukewarm water, melted butter, beaten egg, sugar, and salt in a medium (large if mixing by Hand) bowl, or use the bread pan fitted with the kneading paddle if utilizing the Bread Machine.
- Flour Mix: In a bowl, combine flour and onion powder.

NOTE: For a soft, buttery crust, skip the egg white and brush buns with melted butter just before baking, and right after removing them from the oven.

Bread Machine
- Place the Liquid Mix in the bread pan fitted with kneading paddle and then cover with the Flour Mix. Make a shallow hole in the center and put in the yeast.

- Place the bread pan in the bread maker. Press *Menu* and select *Dough Cycle*. Select *1* lb (*400g* flour) or *2* lb (*800g* flour). Press *Start* to mix, knead, and rise. Total Time = *1:25* for *1* lb loaf; *1:40* for *2* lb loaf. You will need to assist the mixing and kneading, especially if you are preparing the *800g* of flour formula. It will initially be a gnarly and sticky mass but with assistance it will tighten up in about *15* minutes. It will eventually be supple and smooth.

- **For *400g* total flour**: When Cycle is complete, gently punch down dough and turn out on a floured work surface. Turn the bread machine off. ***Go To Prep & Shape.***

- **For *800g* total flour**: When mixing/kneading is done (*1:05* on timer), remove the dough from the bread pan and turn out on a floured surface. Turn the bread machine off. Remove the kneading paddle (if stuck into the dough) and shape the dough into a ball. Place in the oiled bowl (large enough to handle the doubling of the dough), and turn to coat all of the dough. Cover with plastic wrap and place in a warm place to rise for *45-60* minutes, or until just about double in bulk.

- When ready, gently punch down dough and turn out on a floured work surface.

Prep & Shape
- Divide dough into the desired number of equal pieces and make them into little dough balls, and cover and let rest for *15* minutes.
NOTE: When making for a buffet lunch or similar setting, I make each roll 56g.

Bun Shape
Pat or roll dough into a *12" x 17"* rectangle. *Sprinkle the dough with the minced onion and press it gently into the surface.*

- Starting with the short (*12"*) end, roll the dough into a log, sealing the ends and side seam. Cut the log into eight slices.

Alternative
Shape rolls as you do for Kaiser, but no stamp of course. Divide into equal pieces (*8 or 16*). Flatten each piece; about *4 to 6"* diameter. Cover with minced onions, and pat into dough. Roll into a ball. I make ball sizes to equal desired number of buns.

Next
- Place the buns on a lightly greased or parchment-lined baking sheet, flattening them to about *3"* wide. Cover them and allow them to rise till they're very puffy, about *1* hour. Preheat the oven to *375°F/190.6°C*.

Prep & Bake
- Uncover the buns, brush them with the <u>beaten egg</u> <u>white/water</u> (or <u>butter</u>), and sprinkle with <u>seeds</u>, if desired.

- Bake for *18-20* minutes, until they're golden brown and feel set when you poke them. Remove from the oven and cool on a wire rack. When completely cool, wrap in plastic, and store at room temperature.

Notes

Parker House Rolls

Bread Machine		
A	P	Action
5		Preparation
15		Assemble & Weigh
5	100	Dough Prep
	----	1st Rise
20		Shaping
10	60	2nd Rise
10	60	Final Rise
10	30	Bake
5	30	Cool
80	280	TOTAL
1:20	4:40	6 hrs 0 min

Invented in 19th century at the Parker House Hotel in Boston, the dough was flattened into an oval and then folded in half. They are soft & buttery with a crispy crust. A bit of trivia ... they also created the Boston Cream Pie.

Recipe from a magazine; unidentifiable now.

%	Ingredient	Volume	Grams	Volume	Grams
		~15 Rolls	**437.5**	~27 Rolls	**800.0**
54.86	Milk	1C	240.0	1 3/4c+1Tb	438.88
8.231	Granulated sugar	3Tbs	36.0	1/3C	65.85
25.92	Unsalted butter	1Stick	113.4	3/4c+2Tb+2tsp	207.36
10.74	Egg; beaten	1Large	47.0	1 Large + 1 small	85.92
2.06	Salt	1 1/2tsp	9.0	1Tb	16.48
100.0	All-purpose flour	3 1/2C	437.5	6 1/3C	800.0
1.6	Active dry yeast	2 1/4tsp	7.0	4 1/8tsp	12.8
203.41	**TOTAL**		**889.9**		**1627.29**
	Topping				
19.44	Sharp cheddar cheese; shredded	3/4C	85.05	1 1/3C+2tsp	155.52
0.55	Old Bay seasoning	1tsp	2.4		4.4

Hydration = (438.88g+85.92g)/800g = 524.8g/800g = .656 or 65.6%

Preparation

- Be sure to review the formula, and your machine's requirements before proceeding.
- Assemble and weigh/measure all ingredients. It will make your work much easier to have all weighed/measured and ready to follow directions.
- In a microwave-safe cup, heat the <u>milk</u> until warm but not hot, about *20* seconds

Rolls 121

- Soften/melt *6* of the *8* Tablespoons (remaining *2* tablespoons will be melted and used later) of the butter in the microwave (about *20* seconds).
- Beat the egg(s).
- Liquid Mix: Mix the milk, sugar, melted butter, beaten egg, and salt in a medium (large if mixing by Hand) bowl, or use the bread pan fitted with the kneading paddle if utilizing the Bread Machine.

Bread Machine

- Place the Liquid Mix in the bread pan fitted with kneading paddle and then cover with the flour. Make a shallow hole in the center and put in the yeast.

- Place the bread pan in the bread maker. Press *Menu* and select *Dough Cycle*. Select *1* lb (*437.5g* flour) or *2* lb (*800g* flour). Press *Start* to mix, knead, and rise. Total Time = *1:25* for *1* lb loaf; *1:40* for *2* lb loaf.

- If you are making the small formula (*437.5g* flour) then the dough can remain in the machine for its rise. However, if you are making the large formula (*800g* total flour) then you **must** remove the dough after mixing/kneading is done, and place it in an oiled bowl large enough to handle the dough doubling in size.

- **For *437.5g* total flour**: When Cycle is complete, gently punch down dough and turn out on a floured work surface. Turn the bread machine off. ***Go To Prep & Shape.***

- **For *800g* total flour**: When mixing/kneading is done (*1:05* on timer), remove the dough from the bread pan and turn out on a floured surface. Turn the bread machine off. Remove the kneading paddle (if stuck into the dough) and shape the dough into a ball. Place in the oiled bowl (large enough to handle the doubling of the dough), and turn to coat all of the dough. Cover with plastic wrap and place in a warm place to rise for *45- 60* minutes, or until just about double in bulk.

- When ready, gently punch down dough and turn out on a floured work surface.

Prep & Shape

For Large Formula: Divide dough in half and prepare each half according to the following.

- Pat it into a *10*-inch square. Fold *one-third* of the dough into the center and the other *third* on top, like folding a letter. Turn the dough and fold again; you should have a small square. Butter the bowl and return the dough to it. Cover with plastic wrap and let stand in a warm place until doubled in bulk, about *1* hour.

- Grease a *9-by-13*-inch baking sheet, or line it with parchment paper.

- *Traditional Shape*: Divide into desired sizes and then form each into a roll. Flatten each roll into an oblong shape, and then fold it in half. Place on prepared baking sheet.

- *Alternative Shape*: On a well-floured work surface, roll out the dough to a *15*-inch square. Working from the bottom, tightly roll the dough into a log. Using a floured knife, cut the log into *thirds*. Cut each *third* into *5* slices. Arrange the rolls spiral side up in the prepared baking sheet in *3* rows of *5*.

- Cover loosely with oiled plastic wrap and let rise for about *1* hour, until billowy. Preheat the oven to *375°F/190.6°C*.

Prep & Bake

- Remove the plastic wrap and bake the rolls for *15* minutes.

- Remove from oven and sprinkle the cheddar cheese on top and bake for *15* minutes longer, until golden and cooked through; cover the rolls with foil for the last *5* minutes to prevent over-browning.

- Remove from the oven and brush the rolls with the remaining *2* tablespoons of melted butter and sprinkle them with the Old Bay seasoning. Transfer the baking pan to a rack to let the rolls cool before serving.

- *Make Ahead*: The baked rolls can be kept at room temperature overnight. Re-warm before serving.

Notes

Pumpernickel Raisin Rolls

Bread Machine		
A	P	Action
5		Preparation
15		Assemble & Weigh
10	35	Dough Prep
	60	1st Rise
20	15	Shaping
	60	Final Rise
5	15	Bake
5	30	Cool
60	215	TOTAL
1:00	3:35	4 hrs 35 min

This is based on the Pumpernickel Raisin Walnut Bread, without the walnuts. It was easily sized down by using the Baker's Percentage.

%	Ingredient	Volume	Grams	Volume	Grams
			400.0		**800.0**
60.0	Water	1C+1Tbs	240.0	2C+2Tbs	480.0
1.875	Salt	1 1/4tsp	7.5	2 1/2tsp	15.44
18.35	Molasses	3Tb+1 1/4tsp	73.4	1/3C+1Tbs+1 1/2tsp	146.8
3.5	Vegetable oil	1Tbs	14.0	1Tbs+2 1/2tsp	28.0
67.5	Unbleached white bread flour	2 1/4C	270.0	4 1/2C	540.0
13.0	Whole-wheat flour	1/3C+1tbs+2tsp	52.0	3/4C+2Tbs	104.0
10.0	Rye flour	1/3C+1Tbs	40.0	3/4C1tsp+3/4tsp	80.0
9.5	Cornmeal	1/4C+2 1/4tsp	38.0	1/2C+1tsp	76.0
3.125	Vital wheat gluten	1Tbs+2Tsp	12.5	3Tbs+1Tsp	25.0
2.5	Unsweetened cocoa powder	2Tbs	10.0	1/4C	20.0
0.885	Instant espresso powder	2tsp	3.54	1Tbs+1tsp	7.08
1.50	Rapid rise yeast	1 3/4tsp	6.0	1Tbs+3/4tsp	12.0
21.32	raisins	1/2C+1Tbs+1/2tsp	85.28	1C+2Tbs+1tsp	170.56
1.333	Caraway seeds	2tsp	5.33	1Tbs+1tsp	10.66
214.39	**TOTAL**		**857.77**		**1715.54**

Hydration = 480g/(540g+104g+80g+76g) = 480g/800g = .60 or 60.0%

400g of flour yields 6 (112g), 8 (84g), 10(67g), 12 (56g) rolls
800g of flour yields 12 (142g), or 16 (107g), 24(71g) rolls

Preparation

- Be sure to review the formula, and your machine's requirements before proceeding.
- Assemble and weigh/measure all ingredients. It will make your work much easier to have all weighed/measured and ready to follow directions.
- Ensure Water at *80°F/26.7°C – 90°F/32.2°C*.
- Liquid Mix: Mix warm water, salt, molasses, and vegetable oil in a medium (large if mixing by Hand) bowl, or use the bread pan fitted with the kneading paddle if utilizing the Bread Machine.
- Flour Mix: Mix flours with vital wheat gluten, cornmeal, cocoa powder, and espresso powder.

Bread Machine

- Place the Liquid Mix in the bread pan fitted with kneading paddle and then cover with the Flour Mix. Make a shallow hole in the center and put in the yeast.

- Place the bread pan in the bread maker. Press *Menu* and select *Dough Cycle*. Select *1* lb (*400g* flour) or *2* lb (*800g* flour). Press *Start* to mix, knead, and rise. Total Time = *1:25* for *1* lb loaf; *1:40* for *2* lb loaf. You will need to assist the mixing and kneading, especially if you are preparing the *800g* of flour formula. It will initially be a gnarly and sticky mass but with assistance it will tighten up in about *15* minutes. It will eventually be supple and smooth.

- When Mix-in's tone sounds (*1 lb loaf = 1:12; 2 lb loaf = 1:19 Remaining*) add raisins and caraway seeds. I have found that I need to monitor the "gathering" of the raisins and caraway seeds. I use a spatula to aid the dough in taking up the ingredients. I have even paused the machine. to spread the dough a bit and turned it back on. Just be sure that all added ingredients have been mixed well.

- **For *400g* total flour**: When Cycle is complete, gently punch down dough and turn out on a floured work surface. Turn the bread machine off. ***Go To Prep & Shape.***

- **For *800g* total flour**: When mixing/kneading is done (*1:05* on timer), remove the dough from the bread pan and turn out on a floured surface. Turn the bread machine off. Remove the kneading paddle (if stuck into the dough) and shape the dough into a ball. Place in the oiled bowl (large enough to handle the doubling of the dough), and turn to coat all of the dough. Cover with plastic wrap and place in a warm place to rise for *45- 60* minutes, or until just about double in bulk.

- When ready, gently punch down dough and turn out on a floured work surface.

Prep & Shape

- Divide dough into the desired number of equal pieces and make them into little dough balls, and cover and let rest for *15* minutes. *NOTE: When making for a buffet lunch or similar setting, I make each roll 56g.*

- Shape the pieces into round balls, and place them on a parchment lined baking sheet. The size/weight of each ball will determine the number for this batch.

- Cover the rolls, and allow them to rise for *45* minutes to *1* hour, or until they've almost doubled in volume. Meanwhile, preheat oven to *450°F/232.2°C*.

Prep & Bake

- Dock (slash) the tops of the rolls with a sharp knife, making an X on each. Brush or spritz the tops with <u>milk</u>. Place rolls in preheated oven, close the door and reduce the temperature to *425°F/218.3°C*. Bake for *13 to 15* minutes (*It may be a bit longer if baking the large batch*), or until they're golden brown. You may need to turn the trays if your oven doesn't heat evenly.

- Remove them from the oven, and cool on a wire rack.

Notes

TJ's Extra Special Crescent

> Strong & lasting friendships provided the key ingredient in the development of this formula. We predict it will become one of your favorite rolls.

Bread Machine		
A	P	Action
5		Preparation
15		Assemble & Weigh
5	100	Dough Prep
	----	1st Rise
25		Shaping
	60	Final Rise
5	14	Bake
5	0	Cool
55	174	TOTAL
0:55	2:54	3 hrs 49 min

Contributor: Teresa Roberts & Tina Jessee

%	Ingredient	Volume	Grams	Volume	Grams
		16 Rolls	**322.0**	**32 Rolls**	**644.0**
45.36	water	1/2C +1 1/2Tbs	134.66	1C+3Tbs	269.33
18.8	Egg; beaten	1Large	47.0	2 large	94.0
1.2	Salt	1/2tsp	3.0	1tsp	6.0
19.2	Sugar	1/4C	48.0	1/2C	96.0
19.0	Vegetable shortening; melted	1/4C	47.5	1/2C	95.0
100.0	White bread flour	2C+2/3C +1tsp	322.0	5C+1/3 +1 1/2tsp	644.0
2.8	Rapid rise yeast	2 1/4tsp	7.0	1Tbs +1 1/2tsp	14.0
214.81	TOTAL		609.165		1218.33
	Unsalted butter; melted; *For Brushing*	2 Tbs	28.35	1/4C	56.7

Hydration = (269.33g+94g)/644g = 363.33g/644g = .5642 or 56.42%

Preparation

- Be sure to review the formula, and your machine's requirements before proceeding.
- Assemble and weigh/measure all ingredients. It will make your work much easier to have all weighed/measured and ready to follow directions.
- Ensure <u>water</u> at *80°F/26.7°C*.

Rolls 129

- Melt/soften <u>shortening</u> in microwave (about 45 sec. Don't forget to cover with paper towel).
- In a small bowl, beat the <u>egg(s)</u> well.
- <u>Liquid Mix</u>: Mix the <u>warm water</u>, <u>salt</u>, <u>sugar</u>, <u>melted shortening</u>, and <u>beaten egg</u> in a medium (large if mixing by Hand) bowl, or use the bread pan fitted with the kneading paddle if utilizing the Bread Machine.

Bread Machine

- In the bread machine pan fitted with the kneading paddle, add <u>Liquid Mix</u>. Cover with the <u>flour</u> and make a shallow hole in the center and put in the <u>yeast</u>. Place the bread pan in the bread maker. Press *Menu* and select *Dough Cycle*. Select *1* lb (*322g* flour) or *2* lb (*644g* flour). Press *Start* to mix, knead, and rise. Total Time = *1:25* for *1* lb loaf; *1:40* for *2* lb loaf. Use a spatula, and be ready to assist in the mixing and kneading.

- When dough cycle is complete, remove dough and place onto a floured surface, and gently punch down.

Prep & Shape

- Divide into two or four portions depending on small or large formula. Roll each to a *12*-inch circle on a floured surface; spread with <u>melted butter</u> and cut each circle into eight wedges. I use a pizza cutter and cut it just like a pizza. Roll up each wedge and place on lightly greased or parchment lined baking sheet. Cover and let rise in a warm place for *1* hour or doubled in bulk. If removing from freezer, leave at room temperature for about one hour.

- Preheat oven to *400°F/204.4°C*.

Bake

- Bake at *400°F/204.4°C* for *11-14* minutes. before serving. Remove and serve hot.

- If eating later, under bake about *5* minutes (Just before rolls start to brown), remove and let cool. Once cooled, they can be placed in a sealed plastic bag and stored in the refrigerator to be used next day, or placed in the freezer for longer storage.

Notes

Appendix One: Cuisinart CBK-200
For Reference Only

Cuisinart CBK 200							
Basic White	Light		Medium		Dark	
Size; lbs	1.5	2.0	1.5	2.0	1.5	2.0
Preheat	0						
Knead1	3						
Knead2	31						
Rise1	26						
Knead3	15 sec						
Rise2	25						
Knead4	15 sec						
Rise3	55						
Total Rise	1:46						
Bake	0:40	0:43	0:50	0:55	1:05	1:10
Total	3:00	3:03	3:10	3:15	3:25	3:30
Keep warm	1:00						
mix-ins	0:20						
Remove paddle	1:25						

Cuisinart CBK 200							
French Italian	Light		Medium		Dark	
Size; lbs	1.5	2.0	1.5	2.0	1.5	2.0
Preheat	0						
Knead1	3						
Knead2	30						
Rise1	32						
Knead3	15 sec						
Rise2	30						
Knead4	15 sec						
Rise3	55						
Total Rise	1:57						
Bake	0:53	1:04	1:06	1:10	1:12	1:14
Total	3:23	3:34	3:36	3:40	3:42	3:44
Keep warm	1:00						
mix-ins	0:19						
Remove paddle	1:35						

Cuisinart CBK 200							
Whole Wheat	Light		Medium		Dark	
Size; lbs	1.5	2.0	1.5	2.0	1.5	2.0
Preheat	30						
Knead1	3						
Knead2	25						
Rise1	80						
Knead3	15 sec						
Rise2	31						
Knead4	15 sec						
Rise3	46						
Total Rise	2:37						
Bake	0:44	0:48	0:50	0:55	1:00	1:04
Total	4:19	4:23	4:25	4:30	4:35	4:39
Keep warm	1:00						
mix-ins	0:44						
Remove paddle	2:49						

Cuisinart CBK 200							
Sweet Breads	Light		Medium		Dark	
Size; lbs	1.5	2.0	1.5	2.0	1.5	2.0
Preheat	0						
Knead1	3						
Knead2	31						
Rise1	31						
Knead3	15 sec						
Rise2	30						
Knead4	15 sec						
Rise3	50						
Total Rise	1:51						
Bake	0:54	0:56	0:57	1:00	1:01	1:04
Total	3:19	3:21	3:22	3:25	3:26	3:29
Keep warm	1:00						
mix-ins	0:20						
Remove paddle	1:55						

Appendix One: Cuisinart CBK-200
For Reference Only

	Cuisinart		
Dough Cycle	1 lb	1.5 lb	2 lb
Rest	0	0	0
Knead1&2	27	30	35
Rise1	58	60	65
Rise2	x	x	x
Rise3	x	x	x
Total Rise	58	60	65
Bake	x	x	x
Total	1:25	1:30	1:40
Keep warm	x	x	x
Add ins	13	16	21
Remove paddle	x	x	x

Appendix Two: Citations & References

Citations
Delicious Direct Breads

page 1: Serge Doucette and Bettina Doucette, *Mastering Sourdough: Trapping, Taming & Training Wild Yeast* (Self Published. Printed by CreateSpace, Charleston, 2018), 6.

page 2: Doucette, Serge and Bettina Doucette. *Bread Defined: Terms, Tips & Troubleshooting.* Self Published. Printed by CreateSpace, Charleston, 2018.

page 2: Serge Doucette and Bettina Doucette, *Mastering Sourdough: Trapping, Taming & Training Wild Yeast* (Self Published. Printed by CreateSpace, Charleston, 2018), 7.

page 4: Doucette and Doucette, *Bread Defined*, 6.

page 5: Doucette and Doucette, *Bread Defined*. 2018, 74.

page 6: "English Muffin Bread," *kingarthurflour.com*, Last Accessed 11/10/2017, http://search.kingarthurflour.com/ search?w=english%20muffin%20bread&af=type:recipes

page 10: Definitions from: Doucette and Doucette, *Bread Defined*. 2018, 55.

page 14: "English Muffin Bread," *kingarthurflour.com*, Last Accessed 11/10/2017, http://search.kingarthurflour.com/ search?w=english%20muffin%20bread&af=type:recipes

page 18: Farmhouse Loaf: From: http://www.macmillandictionary.com/dictionary/british/farmhouse-loaf

page 24: Ingram, Christine, and Jennie Shapter. *The Complete Book of Bread & Bread Machines.* London: Hermes House, 2002, 2008.

page 27: "100% Whole Wheat Bread For The Bread Machine," *kingarthurflour.com*, Last Accessed 11/10/2017, https://www.kingarthurflour.com/recipes/100-whole-wheat-bread-for-the-bread-machine-recipe

page 32: Christine Ingram and Jennie Shapter. *The Complete Book of Bread & Bread Machines.* (London: Hermes House, 2002, 2008), 356.

page 41: CBK-200 Cuisinart Convection Bread Maker; *Recipe Booklet*, 55.

page 51: CBK-200 Cuisinart Convection Bread Maker; *Recipe Booklet*, 50.

page 58: CBK-200 Cuisinart Convection Bread Maker; *Recipe Booklet*, 19.

page 68: " Paular "Cranberry Orange Breakfast Bread," *allrecipes.com*, Last Accessed 11/10/2017,http://allrecipes.com/ Recipe/ Cranberry-Orange-Breakfast-Bread/Detail.aspx?event8=1&prop24=SR_Title&e11=cranberry%20orange%20walnut%20bread&e8=Quick%20Search&event10=1&e7=Recipe&soid=sr_results_p1i2

page 72: "Hot Cross Buns," *foodnetwork.com*, Last Accessed 11/10/2017, http://www.foodnetwork.com/recipes/food-network-kitchen/hot-cross-buns-recipe-1928112#!

page 79: "German Stollen Recipe," *tasteofhome.com*, Last Accessed 11/10/2017, http://www.tasteofhome.com/recipes/ german-stollen

page 93: Marie Lupo Tusa, *Marie's Melting Pot.* ISBN 0960706291, T & M Pubns, 1980.

page 94: "Olive Salad," *myrecipes.com*, Last Accessed 11/10/2017, http://www.myrecipes.com/recipe/olive-salad-10000000522564/

page 102: Guy Fieri "Stromboli," *foodnetwork.com*, Last Accessed 11/10/2017, http://www.foodnetwork.com/recipes/guy-fieri/stromboli-recipe-2124726

page 106: *Southern Living 2000 Annual Recipes*. (Birmingham: Oxmoor House, Inc. Book Division of Southern Progress Corporation, 2000), 257.

page 109: "Kaiser Rolls," *kingarthurflour.com*, Last Accessed 11/10/2017, http://www.kingarthurflour.com/recipes/kaiser-rolls-recipe

page 113: "Norm's Onion Rolls," thefreshloaf.com, Last Accessed 11/10/2017, http://www.thefreshloaf.com/recipes/ normsonionrolls

page 117: "Onion Buns, Published: 01/01/2010," *kingarthurflour.com*, Last Accessed 11/10/2017, http://www.kingarthurflour.com/recipes/onion-buns-recipe

Appendix Two: Citations & References

All Of Our Books
References

The following is representative of the various sources I have utilized in the writings of our books. I have made every attempt to be all-inclusive, and any omissions I may have made were unintentional and will be corrected when identified.

Publications

- 52 Loaves; William Alexander; Algonquin Books Of Chapel Hill, 2010.
- Amy's Bread; Amy Scherber & Kim Dupree; William Morrow and Company, Inc. New York; 1996.
- Artisan Baking Across America; The Breads, The Bakers, The Best Recipes; Maggie Glezer; Artisan, New York; 2000.
- Baker's Percentage and Formula Weights; Vancouver Community College; http://library.vcc.ca/learningcentre/pdf/vcclc/BakersMath-PercentagesAndFormulaWeights.pdf
- Bread Baker's Of America; Bread Lines; Formatting Guild Formulas; bbga.org; 2009.
- Classic Sourdoughs (revised) A Home Baker's Handbook, Ed Wood and Jean Wood; 10 Speed Press, Berkeley, 2001.
- Cookwise the hows and whys of successful cooking; Shirley O. Corriher; William Morrow and Company, Inc., New York; 1997.
- Crust and Crumb: Master Formulas For Serious Bread Baker's; Peter Reinhart; Ten Speed Press, Berkeley/Toronto; 2006.
- Cuisinart Convection Bread Machine; Model CBK200; Recipe Booklet; IB-5859D.
- The Fannie Farmer Cookbook; Eleventh Edition; Revised by Wilma Lord Perkins; Little, Brown and Company, Boston/Toronto; 1965.
- Great Breads: Home Baked Favorites from Europe, the British Isles & North America; Martha Rose Shulman; Chapters Publishing Ltd., Shelburne, Vermont 05482; 1995.
- Kneadlessly Simple Fabulous, Fuss-Free, No-Knead Breads; Nancy Baggett; John Wiley & Sons. Inc. Hoboken, New Jersey; 2009.
- Nancy Silverton's Breads From The La Brea Bakery, Recipes for the Connoisseur; Nancy Silverton in collaboration with Laurie Ochoa; Villard, New York, 1996.
- Real Bread A fearless guide to making it; Maggie Bayliss & Coralie Castle, 101 Productions San Francisco; 1980.
- the bread bible; Rose Levy Beranbaum; W.W. Norton & Company, New York, London; 2003.
- The Bread Machine Cookbook; Donna Rathmell German, Bristol Publishing enterprises, Inc., San - Leandro, California; 1991.
- The Complete Book Of Bread & Bread Machines; Christine Ingram and Jennie Shapter; Hermes House 2008.
- The Village Baker; Classic Regional Breads from Europe and America; Joe Ortiz; Ten Speed Press; Berkeley, California; Paperback; 1997.
- Zojirushi, How To Enjoy Your Home Bakery Virtuoso Breadmaker; Model BB-PAC20; Operating Instructions & Recipes.

Websites
Dictionary

- https://www.merriam-webster.com/
- http://www.dictionary.com/
- http://www.thefreedictionary.com/
- https://www.urbandictionary.com/define.php?term=sourdough

Appendix Two: Citations & References

General/Miscellaneous
- https://www.allrecipes.com/
- https://www.kingarthurflour.com/
    - https://blog.kingarthurflour.com/
- https://www.mccormick.com/
- http://www.myrecipes.com/
- https://www.tasteofhome.com/
- http://www.kraftrecipes.com/
- http://www.theartisan.net
- http://www.thefreshloaf.com/forum
- https://www.thekitchn.com/
- https://www.youtube.com/
- https://en.wikipedia.org
- https://www.yummly.com/

Baker's Percentage
- https://www.craftybaking.com/howto/bakers-percentage-method
- http://hotchef.ning.com/page/bakers-percentage
- https://bread-magazine.com/bakers-percentage/
- https://www.weekendbakery.com/posts/bakers-percentage-demystified/
- https://www.bbga.org/bread/bakers_percentage
- https://www.bbga.org/files/BakersPercent-Healea.pdf
- http://theartisan.net/BPercent.htm
- https://thebakersguide.com/the-bakers-percentage
- http://www.wildyeastblog.com/bakers-percentage-1/
- http://artisanbreadbaking.com/school/bakers-percentage/
- http://www.wildyeastblog.com/bakers-percentage-2/
- https://stellaculinary.com/cooking-videos/stella-bread/sb-001-what-bakers-percentage
- http://www.thefreshloaf.com/handbook/baker039s-math
- http://www.kvalifood.com/page/bread-baking-technique-1-the-baker-s-percentage/uuid/c205f17d-4f7c-11e6-8a98-1ccb1ab7d52c
- http://microbaker.yolasite.com/bakers-percentage-calculator.php
- https://www.pizzatoday.com/departments/in-the-kitchen/bakers-percentage/

Yeast/LAB/Respiration/Fermentation
- http://www.dictionary.com/browse/yeast
- http://www.breadworld.com/
- http://www.dakotayeast.com/home.html
- http://fleischmannsyeast.com/
- https://instruction.bact.wisc.edu/instr/book/displayarticle/95
- https://www.khanacademy.org/science/biology/cellular-respiration-and-fermentation/variations-on-cellular-respiration/a/fermentation-and-anaerobic-respiration
- https://www.khanacademy.org/science/biology/cellular-respiration-and-fermentation/variations-on-cellular-respiration/v/lactic-acid-fermentation
- https://www.khanacademy.org/science/biology/cellular-respiration-and-fermentation/variations-on-cellular-respiration/a/connections-between-cellular-respiration-and-other-pathways

Appendix Two: Citations & References

- https://www.khanacademy.org/science/biology/cellular-respiration-and-fermentation/variations-on-cellular-respiration/a/regulation-of-cellular-respiration
- https://metacyc.org/META/new-image?type=PATHWAY&object=P122-PWY
- http://www.pmbio.icbm.de/lehre/ws1011/vlphys/vlphys-09.pdf
- http://redstaryeast.com/
- http://www.rsc.org/learn-chemistry/resource/res00000470/fermentation-of-glucose-using-yeast?cmpid=CMP00005115
- http://textbookofbacteriology.net/lactics.html
- https://whatscookingamerica.net/Bread/yeastbreadtip.htm
- https://en.wikipedia.org/wiki/Lactic_acid_fermentation
- https://en.wikipedia.org/wiki/Lactobacillus
- https://en.wikipedia.org/wiki/Lactobacillus_pontis
- https://en.wikipedia.org/wiki/Lactobacillus_sanfranciscensis
- https://en.wikipedia.org/wiki/Yeast
- http://www.thefreshloaf.com/node/10375/lactic-acid-fermentation-sourdough; Debra Wink; January 19, 2009
- https://en.wikipedia.org/wiki/Fermentation
- https://en.wikipedia.org/wiki/Lactic_acid
- https://en.wikipedia.org/wiki/Phytic_acid

Sourdough

- http://www.alaska.net/~logjam/Sourdough.html
- http://www.angelfire.com/ab/bethsbread/WhatisSourdough.html
- https://www.culturesforhealth.com/
- https://www.epicurious.com/
- http://www.geniuskitchen.com/recipe/sourdough-bread-starter-13750
- https://www.instructables.com/
- https://nourishedkitchen.com/how-to-make-a-sourdough-starter/
- https://www.nytimes.com/2016/03/23/dining/sourdough-starter-bread-baking.html
- http://pinchmysalt.com/
- http://ranprieur.com/misc/sourdough.html
- http://www.sourdo.com/
- https://sourdough.com/
- https://www.sourdoughhome.com/
- https://www.theguardian.com/lifeandstyle/2014/mar/08/make-your-own-sourdough-bread-starter-recipe
- https://www.theperfectloaf.com/7-easy-steps-making-incredible-sourdough-starter-scratch/
- https://whatscookingamerica.net/Bread/SourdoughStarter.htm
- https://en.wikipedia.org/wiki/Pre-ferment
- https://en.wikipedia.org/wiki/Sourdough
- https://en.wikipedia.org/wiki/Sponge_and_dough
- https://en.wikipedia.org/wiki/Straight_dough

Made in the USA
Columbia, SC
07 April 2018